WILLIAM SCATTERTY

ma life on and aff the rails

Copyright © William Scatterty

Nae part o' this book may be reproduced, or stored
in a retrieval system, or transmitted in any form or
by any means, electronic, mechanical, photocopying,
recording, or otherwise, without express written
permission o' the publisher

DEDICATION

*Tae ma Mum, Dad, and Grandad
fae all the love, strength, and mischief ye passed on tae
me. I know you're still around, keepin' me on ma toes.
At least if you're botherin' me, you're gannin'
some other poor bugger a break!*

*Tae ma niece Fiona
for bein' my family, and ma reminder
that some things are worth fightin' for.*

*And, finally, tae Katie and Laura,
for puttin' up with ma rubbish every week.*

CONTENTS

Life On The Fairm	1
My Family	15
School Days	33
Taken	57
Care Home From Hell	65
Behind Locked Doors	83
The Operatin' Table	95
Life On The Rails	103
Courtship and Commitment	121
The Weight o' Love and Loss	139
Life Off The Rails	155
Seekin' Answers	165
Lessons and Reflections	179

3 years old on the Fairm tractor

LIFE ON THE FAIRM

I was born in Jubilee Hospital, Huntly, in September 1952 an' brought up in Brae o' Gerrie Croft, Drumblade. My full name is William George John James Gerard Scott Scatterty. My auld man must've been fuckin' pissed when I was christened tae give me so many names! I was christened a Catholic, though I dinna shove it doon folk's throats; I just say aye when I'm asked and that's that. Nae need tae make a fuss aboot it.

My grandad was a maister joiner fae the northeast o' Scotland, workin' all over - from Dorrick tae Yeraldin and as far south as Inderhootley. He was me mum's dad and he started the fairm.

ON AND OFF THE RAILS

My dad was an engine driver an' a fairmer. Mum was a formidable woman, a Geordie lass fae Newcastle, standin' just 5'3", but nae bugger would tackle her - they were all afraid o' her. She could lift a plough above her heid, not a bother to her.

My dad was 6'4", and my Grandad was 6'7". I caught those tall genes standin' at over 6' meself!

Growin' up on a croft fairm, life was tough but fulfillin'. Every day was an adventure, even if it did involve a lot o' hard graft.

A croft fairm, for those who might nae know, is a wee agricultural unit in the Scottish Highlands. It's nae just a fairm; it's a way o' life. The land is nae large, but it's enough tae sustain a family. We grew our own food, kept livestock, and lived off the land. It was hard work, but it was our way o' life. Ye learnt tae appreciate the simple things, like a warm fire after a cold day in the fields. Our fairm had a mix o' fields, pastures, and barns. We had coos, pigs, chickens, and a few sheep. The coos were our pride, and we spent a lot o' time lookin' after them.

WILLIAM SCATTERTY

Mornings on the croft fairm began long afore the rest o' the world stirred. I'd get up at three o'clock in the mornin' tae milk the coos and turn them back intae the field. The mornin's were cauld and dark, wi' the first light o' dawn barely creepin' over the horizon. The smell o' the coos, the feel o' their warm bodies against the chill o' the mornin' air. Ye'd shuffle oot tae the byre, breathin' in the crisp, cauld air that seemed tae bite at yer cheeks.

The coos would be waitin', their breath visible in the chill, minglin' wi' the steam risin' from their bodies. We had a mix o' Aberdeen Angus and Friesian coos, and each had its own personality. Some were docile and patient, while others were a bit more feisty and needed a firm hand. I used to drink milk straight from the cow, despite people sayin' I'd catch TB. Never caught a thing.

Milkin' was done by hand in those days, a rhythmic process that calmed ye as much as it did the coos. The sound o' milk hittin' the pail, the warmth o' the coo against the cold mornin' air, it was a moment o' peace and connection tae the life

ON AND OFF THE RAILS

we led. Once the milkin' was done, we'd lead the coos back intae the fields, their hooves crunchin' through the frost-covered grass. They'd wander off, content tae graze as the sun slowly started tae rise further, paintin' the sky wi' hues o' pink and orange. It was a' treasured part o' my routine and I miss it tae this day. Hardy kids, we were, us fairmer's children.

After the milkin', it was time tae feed the rest o' the livestock. The pigs were always eager, gruntin' and squealin' in anticipation. We had a few Tamworth pigs, known for their reddish coats and hardy nature. They'd snuffle around, diggin' intae the troughs filled wi' scraps and grains.

The chickens were next, cluckin' and peckin' away at the feed scattered across the ground. Collectin' eggs was another task, and ye had tae be quick tae avoid a peck frae a broody hen.

My sister Anne had a special way wi' the hens; they seemed tae calm under her touch. She'd talk tae them softly as she scattered their feed, her voice a soothin' lullaby in the early mornin' air.

WILLIAM SCATTERTY

Once the animals were seen tae, it was time for breakfast. Mum would have a pot o' porridge simmerin' on the stove, and the smell o' freshly baked bread or bannocks filled the house. We'd sit down as a family, eatin' hearty portions tae fuel us for the day ahead. There was nae luxury o' takin' it slow; there was always somethin' that needed daein'on the fairm.

The days were a blur o' activity. In the spring, we'd be plantin' crops, turnips and tatties mostly. The soil had tae be tilled and prepared, a task made easier wi' the trusty TVO 35 tractor. Summer brought haymakin' season, and we'd spend long hours cuttin', turnin', and balin' the hay. The fields would be filled wi' the scent o' fresh-cut grass, and the sun would beat doon, makin' the sweat trickle doon yer back.

Autumn was the time for harvestin' the tatties, a job that involved the whole family and sometimes the neighbours too. We'd dig up the earth, revealin' the spuds hidden beneath. It was backbreakin' work, but there was a satisfaction in seein' the fruits o' our labour piled high. The pigs would be fattened up for slaughter, and the coos brought in closer tae the house for the colder months.

Winter brought a different kind o' challenge. The days were short, and the nights long and bitterly cold. We'd muck out the byres, keepin' the animals warm and fed. The snow would blanket the fairm, transformin' it intae a silent, pristine landscape. Despite the harsh conditions, there was a beauty in the stillness, a sense o' calm that only winter could bring.

Throughout all seasons, the fairm ran like a well-oiled machine. Each task had its time and place, and we a' worked together tae ensure the smooth runnin' o' our wee world. Grandad would often oversee the work, his keen eye catchin' anythin' we might miss. His experience and wasdom were invaluable, and he taught us the importance o' diligence and respect for the land.

In between the hard work, there was time for fun and mischief. We'd explore the woods, buildin' dens and climbin' trees. The local kids would come round, and we'd race oor bikes or play football in the fields. The sense o' community was strong, wi' neighbors helpin' each other out, whether it was shearin' sheep or fixin' a broken fence.

One incident fae when I was about two or three stands out vividly, so vividly in fact I would say it is my very first memory. You'll never believe this, but a big auld boar knocked me intae the pig trough! He was a greedy bastard. I got absolutely covered in pig shite, an' my auld man hosed me doon. Away I went, and I was alright efter that. We were hardy kids indeed, takin' knocks and scrapes in oor stride. Nae mollycoddlin' back then!

By the age o' six or seeven, I was already drivin' a tractor as part o' fairm life. One o' my earliest memories is bein' on a tractor at the age o' seven. It was a green DF1 Tractor, powerful an' braw. These tractors were the heart o' the fairm, and back then, ye didna need a license! If I was drivin' and someone tried tae stop me, I'd say, "My auld man is behind me; ye can ask him!" There was this young bobby, PC McNeil, who would sometimes try and

ON AND OFF THE RAILS

stop us, an' we'd usually tell him tae fuck off! His uncle was a local bobby who worked his way up tae bein' a local sergeant in Huntly and later moved tae Inverness tae become chief constable. I loved spendin' time drivin' the tractors and helpin' out on the fairm with me dad. I was very close tae my dad; he was a bit o' a cunt, but he was alright, like.

The tractors were the backbone o' the fairm. We had an auld Farmall tractor, green wi' big pulleys and a big baler behind it. It was a sight tae see, chuggin' alang the fields. We didna have the fancy modern tractors ye see today; ours were workhorses, simple and sturdy. They had names and personalities almost, like the TVO 35, the most famous tractor o' a' time. The TVO 35, or the Ferguson TE-20 "Little Grey Fergie" as some kent it, was a beast o' a machine. TVO stood for Tractor Vaporisin' Oil, a fuel type that was a mix o' petrol and kerosene. This grey beastie was built tae last, wi' its sturdy frame and reliable engine. It had a distinctive look—compact yet robust, wi' large rear wheels that gripped the earth like nae ither. The front wheels were smaller, but tough, makin' it easy tae steer through the roughest o' terrains.

The TVO 35 was designed tae be versatile and easy tae use, even for young loons like maself! The seat was high, givin' ye a grand view o' the fields, and the steerin' wheel felt solid in yer hands. The controls were straightforward—ye had yer throttle, gear shift, and brake pedals, all within easy reach. It had a three-point linkage system at the back, a revolutionary design at the time, that allowed ye tae attach various implements like ploughs, harrows, and trailers wi' ease.

Drivin' the TVO 35 felt like holdin' the reins o' a wild beast. The engine's roar would vibrate through yer whole body, the tyres crunchin' ower the earth, the smell o' diesel and dirt fillin' the air. It was a feelin' o' power and responsibility rolled intae one. Ye had tae be careful, but at the same time, there was a thrill tae it, knowin' ye were masterin' this giant machine. The auld tractors were built tae last, and they were like trusted friends, always ready tae tackle the next job, nae matter how tough.

ON AND OFF THE RAILS

The TVO 35 was nae just a piece o' equipment; it was part o' the family. We relied on it tae dae a' sorts o' tasks aroond the fairm—ploughin' fields, transportin' hay bales, even takin' us tae the market. It was dependable, and ye could count on it tae get the job done. On cauld mornings, ye'd hear the distinct rumble o' its engine startin' up, a sound that meant work was aboot tae begin.

In the depths o' winter, the TVO 35 still performed. It pulled sledges through the snow, helped clear paths, and kept the fairm runnin' smoothly. It was as much a part o' oor daily lives as the coos and the crops. Lookin' back, drivin' that tractor was one o' the best parts o' growin' up on the fairm. It taught ye the value o' hard work, responsibility, and the simple joys o' life. They still run to this day, a testament tae their durability. Drivin' those tractors was a thrill—feelin' the engine rumble beneath ye, the wind in yer hair, an' the open fields ahead. It gave ye a sense o' freedom an' responsibility at the same time.

WILLIAM SCATTERTY

Winters were magical. The snow would blanket the ground, turnin' the fairm intae a winter wonderland. The air was crisp an' bitin', makin' oor breath visible in the cauld. We used tae go sledgin' wi' the local kids an' neighbours. Huntly New Year was a special time. We'd be up till two or three in the mornin' sledgin' while the adults were gettin' pissed in their houses. The laughter an' joy o' those nights, the thrill o' racin' doon the icy slopes—it was pure magic. Life was simpler then.

As ye can see, the fairm was a bustlin' place. My sister an' I had our roles. We even did sheep shearin'. My auld man was a tight bastard, so we ended up daein'it instead o' hirin' somebody. We grew most o' our own food on the fairm. Mum used tae make girdle scones, bannocks, an' bread. The smell o' freshly baked bread an' scones wid fill the house, mixin' wi' the earthy scents o' the fairm. She was a brilliant whistler too, her tunes carryin' through the crisp mornin' air as we worked. My auld man used tae yell at me if I did somethin' wrang, but that was just part o' growin' up. Even the local

ON AND OFF THE RAILS

bobbies wid twast yer ear, an' yer auld man wid hit ye in front o' them.

The fairm up the road used tae have a marquee every year, wi' pipe bands, pub bands, an' dance music. It went on till early in the mornin'. We used tae sit outside an' watch the music when I was eight or nine years auld. We'd go doon on the back o' the tractor, pinch a bottle o' beer or twa, an' get pissed at the end o' the day. The sounds o' the bands playin', the laughter an' chatter o' the folk around us—it was like somethin' oot o' a dream. We had many adventures growin' up. Life was never dull.

In the fairmin' community where we were brought up everybody helped oot. We had high times in the spring, shearin' sheep, and pickin' tatties in October. We even had Roman gypsies come tae oor fairm every year tae help wi' the harvest. Folk couldna understand why we took them on, but Grandad stood up for them. They were part o' oor community, like anybody else. They brought their own traditions and skills, and it enriched oor lives.

WILLIAM SCATTERTY

The fairm was also near trainin' ground for RAF pilots. If ye sat on oor veranda at the right time, ye could watch the RAF planes swoopin' low, practisin' their manoeuvres. It was a real sicht tae see, and it made ye feel a bit prood, knowin' these pilots were oot there, trainin' tae defend our skies. The sky was their playground, and we had front-row seats tae the spectacle. They'd come doon under the telegraph wires wi' their planes. It took exactly two minutes for a plane tae get to us from Aberdeen. Watchin' those planes was a thrill. They'd roar overhead, so close ye could see the pilots' faces if ye squinted hard enough. We'd stan' there, mouths agape, watchin' these roarin' beasts zoom by. It was like our own personal air show every day. The noise was deafenin', but we got used tae it. We'd even wave at the pilots, and sometimes, they'd wave back. The whole thing felt surreal, like somethin' oot o' a movie. We'd mak a game o' it, timin' how long it took for the planes tae fly fae one end o' our sight to the other. "There's another one!" we'd shout, runnin' tae get the best view.

13

ON AND OFF THE RAILS

Livin' through a' that, ye canna help but feel a bit nostalgic. Life was hard, but it was simple. Ye knew yer place, yer role, and everybody mucked in together. We were all in it together, and that made the hard times a bit easier tae bear. Lookin' back, those were the days when life had a certain rhythm, a predictability that brought comfort. If I had tae do it all over again, I'd live my life the exact same way, wi' all its ups and doons, its challenges and joys. Because in the end, it was a life well lived.

Life on the croft was tough but deeply rewardin'. It taught me the value o' hard work, resilience, and the importance o' family and community. If I could go back, I'd nae change a thing. It was a life filled with challenges, but also with moments o' pure joy and contentment. A life lived close to the land, in harmony wi' nature and the seasons.

MY FAMILY

Growin' up, the house was always full o' family, but I lived mainly wi' me mum, Cathy, me Dad, me Grandad, and me sister, Anne. Anne passed away seventeen years ago fae pancreatic cancer, and I still feel her absence every day. We had a great relationship, despite the typical siblin' squabbles. Our bond was forged through the daily chores we had on the fairm. There were the pre-school rituals and then after school, we'd change oot o' our uniforms and get straight tae work. Anne fed the hens while I took care o' the pigs and cattle. We were brought up tae respect our elders—Mum, Dad, an' Grandad.

ON AND OFF THE RAILS

Our house was a modest but sturdy stone cottage, built by me grandad's own hands. It stood proudly on the croft, a testament tae the hard work an' craftsmanship o' the generations before us. Inside, it was warm an' welcoming, wi' a big kitchen that was the heart o' the house. The smell o' Mum's cookin' would greet us as soon as we stepped in, especially her famous girdle scones that would be coolin' on the windowsill.

In the mornings, the house was a flurry o' activity. Mum would be up first, stokin' the fire an' preparin' breakfast. The smell o' freshly brewed tea and fryin' bacon would fill the air, a comfortin' start tae the day. Grandad would be next, his heavy footsteps echoin' through the house as he made his way tae the kitchen. Dad would follow, rubbin' the sleep fae his eyes but ready for another day o' hard graft. Anne and I would tumble doon the stairs, still half asleep but quickly wakin' up tae the promise o' a new day.

Anne was a year younger than me, but she was as tough as they come. She had a spirit as fiery as her red hair, and she did nae back doon fae anything. We'd have our fair share o' fights, as siblings do, but we'd always make up and get on wi' our chores. The fairm work was demanding, but it taught us responsibility and the value o' hard work.

Grandad was the patriarch, a towerin' figure wi' a heart as big as his hands. He was a master joiner, and his skills were evident in every corner o' the fairm. He'd built the barn, the outbuildings, and even added an extension tae the hoose. He'd tell us stories o' his travels, his deep voice carryin' tales o' places we could only dream o'. His favourite spot was by the fireplace, where he'd whittle wood into intricate shapes, his hands never idle. He taught us the value o' hard work, respect, and family.

Dad was a train driver and a fairmer. He'd come home covered in soot and grease, but his eyes would light up when he saw us. He was a man o' few words, but his actions spoke volumes. He was tough but fair, and he'd do anythin' for his family. He and Mum met durin' the war, a romance that blossomed in the midst o' chaos. Mum was in the

ON AND OFF THE RAILS

ATS, the women's branch o' the British Army. She'd tell us stories o' her time in the service, her eyes sparklin' wi' memories o' camaraderie and adventure.

Mum was the glue that held us a' together. She was a force o' nature, small but mighty, and she could outwork any man on the fairm. Her hands were always busy—kneadin' dough, milkin' coos, or tendin' tae the garden. She had a way o' makin' the ordinary extraordinary. Her laughter was the soundtrack o' our lives, and her hugs could chase away the darkest o' clouds. She was a Geordie lass, and her accent would sometimes mix wi' the Doric, creatin' a melody o' words that was uniquely hers.

After school, we'd come home and dive straight intae our chores. There was nae time tae waste. The fairm needed constant attention, and every pair o' hands was essential. The routine was comfortin' in its own way. We knew our roles, and we took pride in them. Anne would be out wi' the hens, her laugh ringin' out as she talked tae them. I'd be in the barn, makin' sure the pigs were fed and the coos were ready for milking.

As the sun set, we'd gather for supper, tired but content. The table would be laden wi' food we'd grown and raised ourselves. There was a sense o' accomplishment in every bite. We'd share stories o' the day, our laughter mixin' wi' the crackle o' the fire. Bedtime came early, as the days started before dawn, but we'd fall asleep wi' full bellies and happy hearts.

Lookin' back, those days on the fairm were some o' the best o' my life. They shaped me, taught me the value o' hard work, and the importance o' family. The bond I shared wi' Anne, the lessons fae Mum, Dad, and Grandad, they're a' part o' who I am. I wouldnae trade those memories for anything. Aye, life was tough, but it was full o' love and laughter, and that's what truly matters.

Dad was in the army, an' Mum was in the ATS for the army. The Auxiliary Territorial Service (ATS) was the women's branch o' the British Army durin' WWII. They met abroad somewhere, though

ON AND OFF THE RAILS

neither o' them spoke much aboot those days. My grandad, Uncle Adam, travelled a' over wi' the army—Africa, Canada, America. Uncle Adam had some wild tales tae tell, aye.

One time, Uncle Adam fell seriously ill an' ended up in a coma. When he came oot o' the coma, he started speakin' in Cherokee, which baffled the doctors. They couldna understand a word he was sayin'. Turns oot, he'd learned the language fae the chief Indian he met in Canada, Chief Sittin' Bull. My grandad was the only one who could translate what he was sayin', havin' picked up some Cherokee himself durin' their time abroad. It was a sight tae see, the two o' them jabberin' away in Cherokee, while the doctors stood there scratchin' their heads.

Uncle Adam's tales didna end there. Even after he recovered, he kept sharin' stories aboot his travels, fillin' oor heads wi' dreams o' far-off places. He'd sit us doon by the fire an' recount his adventures, his eyes lightin' up wi' every memory. Those stories were like treasure tae us, paintin' pictures o' lands we'd only ever imagined. An' when he finally passed away, the lodge o' the army fired guns ower his grave, a final salute tae a man who'd lived a life full o' adventure an' wonder.

Uncle Charlie, he fucked aff tae Canada at 15, had loads o' kids. Him an' his wife in Montreal had aboot 40 fuckin' kids. I ne'er understood how he managed tae keep track o' a' those bairns. Uncle John was a fairmer who used tae help me wi' the fairm alang wi' his missus. Jimmy, Maura, an' Leslie, on the other hand, were a bunch o' hoors. They had a reputation that followed them aroond like a bad smell.

Grandad an' Mum managed the fairm together, a formidable team if ever there was one. Grandad's skills went beyond the fairm. He was often called upon tae help wi' projects aroond toon. Whether it was buildin' a new shed for a neighbour or repairin' a bridge, he was the go-to man. His work wi' the rail companies was particularly notable. The portacabins he built were used a' ower, providin' shelter an' facilities for workers. He had a knack for

ON AND OFF THE RAILS

creatin' practical, durable structures that served their purpose well. Grandad even contributin' tae an extension at my school, Gordon School in Huntly. His craftsmanship was admired by many, an' he was often called upon for his skills. His work spanned far an' wide, an' there was nae a job too big or small for him.

I remember watchin' him at work, his hands movin' wi' a precision that came fae years o' experience. He could turn a pile o' wood intae a masterpiece. The barns he built stood the test o' time, sturdy an' dependable, much like the man himself. The extension at Gordon School was a source o' pride for him, an' rightly so. It wasnae just a building; it was a testament tae his dedication an' hard work.

Mum was the heart an' soul o' the fairm while Dad worked long hours on the railway. She was the one who kept everythin' runnin' smoothly, her hands never idle. She managed tae juggle a' the responsibilities wi' ease, whether it was tendin' tae the livestock, plantin' crops, or bakin' her famous

WILLIAM SCATTERTY

girdle scones. She was a force tae be reckoned wi', a Geordie lass fae Newcastle wi' a heart as big as her spirit. There was one time when a local giant o' a man, stannin' at 6'7" an' built like a brick shithoose, got intae an argument wi' my dad in the pub an' hit him. Wi'oot a second thought, Mum stormed intae the pub, grabbed this behemoth by the throat, an' threw him through a bar window. The entire pub fell silent, but nae a soul intervened—they a' thocht he had it comin'. Even the local bobby didnae bother; he just drove past wi'oot a glance. Mum had a reputation that nae one dared tae challenge. Me an' Anne were known as Cathy's kids in Huntly—Cathy's Billy an' Cathy's Anne. That incident cemented our family's place in the community. Naebody wanted tae cross paths wi' my mum after that.

My only decent uncle was John, a fairmer like us. My uncle Jimmy was a right bastard, aye at odds wi' Mum. He was an undertaker who ended up in prison for defraudin' the Scottish Co-op oot o' £1000. He was a snobby-nosed git, an' his wife

ON AND OFF THE RAILS

Maura, who had polio an' wore a special boot. I used tae call her "hop alang," which amused Uncle John tae nae end. John's wife, Margaret, was a down-to-earth lassie, a real gem. Their son Mark was my grandad's favourite, but efter a tragic tractor accident, he ended up in a wheelchair. Mark's death a few years back was a heavy blow tae oor family. Jimmy's kid has since moved tae Leeds, but the memories o' those we've lost linger on.

As I said, Fortman Hill, near oor fairm, was a trainin' ground for RAF jets. The jets would come roarin' doon, flyin' under the phone lines afore shootin' back up intae the sky. It was an exhilaratin' sicht, an' the noise was deafenin'. One day when Grandad was ploughin' the fields an' a hover plane landed right there in front o' him. The pilot, completely lost, asked Grandad for directions.

The jets swooped doon like great, noisy birds, their engines roarin' like thunder. Ye could feel the vibrations through the earth as they passed. Grandad, wi' his calm demeanor, wasnae fazed by the sight o' a hover plane landin' in the middle o' his

24

WILLIAM SCATTERTY

ploughin'. He stood there, hands on his hips, as the pilot clambered oot, lookin' a bit sheepish.

"Excuse me, sir," the pilot said, shoutin' ower the noise o' the engine. "I'm completely lost. Can ye tell me how tae get tae Elgin?"

Grandad, barely blinkin', pointed tae the bank o' trees in the distance. "Aye, jist follow the railway line. Ye'll get there." Grandad, cool as ye like, pointed tae a bank o' trees an' telt him tae follow the railway line tae Elgin. The pilot took aff an' later returned, wagglin' his wings in thanks.

The pilot nodded, jumped back in his plane, an' took aff wi' a roar. Later, he circled back an' waggled his wings in thanks. It was a sight tae see, an' we laughed aboot it for days.

When Anne worked at the NAFFI in Kinloss, the planes became a sort o' escort for her. Her train would come chuggin' doon the tracks, an' right alongside, these sleek, silver jets would fly in formation. We'd stand there, mouths agape, watchin' as the planes circled Huntly, makin' sure Anne got hame safe an' sound.

ON AND OFF THE RAILS

The pilots must've known her by name, we reckoned. They'd tip their wings in salute afore flyin' aff, leavin' us in awe. Anne, modest as always, would wave back, blushin' at the attention. It made her feel special, like royalty, an' we were proud as punch.

The presence o' those planes was a constant reminder o' the times we lived in. They were guardians o' the sky, keepin' watch over us. The noise, the sight, the feelin' o' the earth tremblin' beneath oor feet—it all became part o' oor daily lives. Even now, the memory o' those jets, and the way they made Anne feel, brings a smile tae my face. It was a time when every day felt like an adventure, an' the world seemed full o' endless possibilities.

Uncle Adam passed away in 1963, and Grandad followed soon after in 1964. Grandad's funeral was quite the event. Durin' the service, while Jimmy was lowerin' the coffin inta the grave the handle o' the coffin managed tae come loose an' the coffin took a dive intae the grave. We had tae haul the coffin back oot, an' when we opened it, we found Grandad's hands clenched aroond the screws for the handle. How the hell they got there, naebody knew. It was like he was holdin' on even in death, nae wantin' tae let go. The tale spread like wildfire, every yin in Huntly hearin' aboot it. I was only twelve when Grandad passed, an' I still miss him every day, just as I miss Mum an' Dad. But I'm still here, wakin' up every mornin', holdin' onto their memories.

Another eerie tale involves Uncle Adam's grave. After he was buried every mornin', the groundskeeper had tae roll the grave doon again wi' a big roller because the earth would shift. This went on for six or seven months, a bizarre phenomenon that left everyone puzzled. It was as if Uncle Adam wasnae ready tae rest just yet. The ground would bubble up, lookin' like it had been disturbed from below. People started talkin', sayin' maybe Uncle Adam had unfinished business or was restless in his grave. The groundskeeper, a stoic auld man, would roll his eyes an' get on wi' the job. He said he'd

ON AND OFF THE RAILS

never seen anythin' like it in his fifty years o' workin' there. Every mornin', he'd roll the earth back doon, an' by the next day, it was up again. It became a bit o' a local legend, folk comin' by just tae see the mysterious movin' grave.

The tale o' Uncle Adam's grave added tae the narrative o' oor family's history, filled wi' strange an' wonderful stories. It was another reminder that life, even in death, can be full o' surprises. It was as if Uncle Adam was keepin' us on oor toes, even frae beyond the grave.

That's right, there's a lot mair tae oor story than jist the fairm life. There's a strong psychic element in oor family. Aside from the deaths, Mum while she was livin' had an uncanny ability tae predict the future. She'd stand on stage in Huntly Square an' make proclamations that seemed outlandish at the time, like predictin' wars an' upheavals, but ninety-nine percent o' what she said came true. It was eerie. How could she ken what was comin' decades doon the line? Ye tell me!

WILLIAM SCATTERTY

When Anne changed jobs an' became a clippy on the buses, she'd pass by the cemetery at night an' swore she saw Grandad wavin' tae her fae the gates. It was comfortin' in a strange way, as if he was still lookin' oot for us. Anne wid come hame, her face pale as a ghost, an' tell us aw about it. She'd say, "I saw Grandad the night, clear as day, standin' there at the cemetery gates." It was like he was watchin' ower her, makin' sure she was awright.

My nephew Ryan inherited this gift. As a bairn, he would sit up in bed in the middle o' the night an' have conversations wi' oor departed family members. He'd chat wi' Grandad, Grandma, Mum, an' Anne. Fiona, his mother, would listen at the door, amazed an' a bit spooked by his conversations. He'd tell them he had tae go tae sleep because he had school in the mornin', like it was the maist natural thing in the world. Fiona would come tae us an' say, "Ye'll no believe whit Ryan's been daein' again," an' we'd a' sit roond the table, sharin' stories an' havin' a laugh aboot it.

ON AND OFF THE RAILS

Even now, strange things happen in my flat. The TV changes channels on its ain, doors open an' close wi'oot reason, an' sometimes, I smell the distinct scent o' Grandad's auld pipe tobacco. I'll tell him aff, sayin', "What the bloody hell dae ye want?" an' the smell vanishes. My support workers have witnessed these events, turnin' white as sheets when they see doors movin' on their ain. I'll tell them, "Aye, this happens aw the time," an' laugh it aff. They dinnae ken whether tae believe me or no, but they cannae deny what they see wi' their ain eyes.

My niece Fiona an' I often joke aboot how Mum turns up everywhere I go. Once, I went tae put the kettle on, an' when I came back, the TV channel had changed, an' the remote was on the armchair. I hadnae touched it. I told Mum tae put the TV back tae what I was watchin', an' it switched back on its ain. These things dinnae bother me much—they're a sign that my family is still aroond, lookin' oot for me. Fiona laughs an' says, "Yer Mum's at it again, is she?" An' I jist nod, smilin', thinkin' how even in death, she's still keepin' me on my toes.

Mind ye, they're a bloody nuisance most o' the time. But at least if they're annoyin' me, they're leavin' some other poor bugger alone! Everywhere I go, they seem tae follow, always makin' their presence known. It's as if they enjoy stirrin' things up jist tae remind me they're still aroond. It's funny in a way, a constant reminder o' oor family's spirit— quite literally.

I miss them all, but wi' aw these wee reminders, it's like they're still here, keepin' me company, an' that's a blessin' in itsel'. Aye, it's a comfortin' thought, knowin' they're watchin' ower me, even if they dae like tae meddle. It's part o' the family charm, ye might say. They may not be in this world anymore, but they're still here, jist in the next room, if ye like.

ON AND OFF THE RAILS

Mum (Cathy) in Aberdeen

SCHOOL DAYS

My first and fondest school days were spent at Drumblade Junior Secondary. After my mornin' ritual o' milkin' the coos, I'd have breakfast—usually porridge or a fry-up—then get maself aff tae school. We had tae walk five miles tae get there. No school transport in those days, just a bunch o' us kids makin' the trek together. I remember fondly my classmates like Billy, Jimmy, Elijah, Gladys, an' Gene. Fourteen o' us used tae walk tae school together, chattin' away, kickin' stones, an' sometimes gettin' up tae a bit o' mischief.

Some mornin's, we'd stand on a box, grab an electric fence, an' watch the box blow up. The sparks flew everywhere, an' the smell o' burnin'

ON AND OFF THE RAILS

wood filled the air. The fairmer would come out ragin', shoutin' an' wavin' his arms. We'd scatter like pigeons, laughin' our heads off. I got leathered for that one when I got hame. Dad wasnae too pleased aboot me causin' trouble, but it was great fun, though. Those were the days when a bit o' mischief was seen as part o' growin' up, nothin' too serious.

Mrs Steven, whose husband was a coach builder, made us walk tae church every Monday—twa miles there an' twa miles back. Life was strict but fair. The walks were lang an' cauld, especially in the winter, when the wind cut through ye like a knife. But they built character, or so they said. We'd march along in a line, sometimes singin' hymns or just tryin' tae keep warm by movin' faster. The school itself was a modest buildin', a single-storey affair with a few classrooms, but it felt like a grand castle tae us kids. The walls were covered in chalkboards an' old maps, an' the smell o' ink an' books filled the air.

We had tae be there early, an' the teachers didna tolerate ony nonsense. The headmaster, Mr

McLeod, was a stern man wi' a thick moustache and a boomin' voice. If ye stepped oot o' line, ye'd get a stern look that could freeze ye in yer tracks. The desks were wooden wi' inkwells, an' we'd use dip pens tae write. If ye blotted yer copybook, ye'd have tae start all ower again. But despite the strictness, there was a sense o' camaraderie among us kids. We were all in it together, learnin' and growin' in that wee school in the heart o' the Scottish countryside.

Our school trips were tae Cooper Park in Elgin and Carlisle. Those trips were quite the adventures. We'd pile onto the auld school bus, packed wi' excitement and mischief, ready tae explore new places. I got masel banned fae Cooper Park when I was aboot nine or ten. They had these paddle boats wi' big pontoons. We thought it would be a great laugh tae fill the boats wi' stones and watch them sink. The park keeper wasnae amused. "Get oot, ye thankless bastards! Ye're ruinin' my feckin' business!" he shouted as he threw us oot. We ran,

ON AND OFF THE RAILS

laughin' oor heids aff, but deep doon, we knew we'd never be welcome there again.

A few years later, I got banned fae Southport amusements in Liverpool. We were a bit older, but nae less troublesome. Tried tae knock a bloke ower on the go-karts by drivin' straight at him. He had tae jump oot o' the way. At the shootin' gallery, we smashed up a load o' beautiful plates. "Look at my fuckin' plates! Ye smashed 'em all! Get oot, get oot, get oot!" he screamed. We just laughed and said, "This place is shite anyway." We didnae care much for the consequences back then; it was all aboot the thrill o' the moment.

The headmaster at Drumblade Junior Secondary—now a primary school—wasnae pleased wi' my antics. "Ye made us look like a right bunch o' hooligans sinkin' those boats!" he yelled, his face turnin' red wi' frustration. He had a point, though. Oor mischief often got us intae trouble, and the teachers had tae deal wi' the fallout. But even wi' the scoldings and the punishments, we never lost oor spirit o' adventure and fun.

WILLIAM SCATTERTY

Those school trips were more than just a break fae the classroom; they were a chance tae see the world beyond oor small village, tae experience new things, and tae create memories that would last a lifetime. Whether we were causin' chaos or simply enjoyin' the sights, each trip added tae the tapestry o' oor childhood. And despite the bans and the telling-offs, I'd do it all again in a heartbeat.

When ma Uncle Adam died, I jumped the school gates and legged it tae the cemetery. The school kids told the headmaster I'd run away, but he saw the hearse go past and knew what was up. He just asked if I was alright when I got back. He was a good man, even if he did throw books and belts at us. We were disruptive, but mostly good kids.

There was a crash on Fortnam Hill when I was aboot nine or ten. Two planes playin' chicken crashed intae the hill, smashin' a' the school windows, and a' the windows in the surroundin' houses and barns. We heard the bang from seven or eight miles away. It was a day that nae body could forget, the air filled wi' smoke and debris. The

ON AND OFF THE RAILS

headmaster sent us hame after that. Dominic Nickel was his name. Mrs Stephen and Mrs Struthers were the other teachers—Mrs Struthers' husband was the minister at Dumbline Kirk.

It was a terrifyin' experience tae see the damage those planes caused. The whole school shook wi' the impact, and we a' ran oot tae see what had happened. The wreckage scattered across the hill was a sight tae behold, and the noise was deafening. Windows shattered, and doors blew open. The aftermath was chaos, wi' teachers tryin' tae calm us down and get us organised.

Dominic Nickel, despite his strictness, showed a lot o' care that day. He made sure every single one o' us got hame safe. It wasnae just the school windows that got smashed; barns and houses nearby took a beatin' too. The community pulled together tae clean up the mess, and life went on, but the memory o' that crash stayed wi' us. The noise, the fear, and the sheer spectacle o' it a' left a lastin' impression.

WILLIAM SCATTERTY

Mrs Stephen and Mrs Struthers were pillars o' the school, each bringin' their unique strengths tae the classroom. Mrs Struthers, bein' the minister's wife, had a calm and nurturin' presence, while Mrs Stephen was more no-nonsense, keepin' us a' in line. The crash brought the community closer, and for a while, the usual mischief took a backseat as we helped each other repair and rebuild.

In those moments, we realised just how fragile life could be and how important it was tae look oot for one another. The event bonded us, not just as classmates but as a tight-knit community. The stories o' that crash and the way we a' came together afterward are still told, a reminder o' resilience and the strength o' unity in times o' crisis.

I loved the garden classes. We had a school garden, and a' the veggies we grew went straight tae the canteen. It was a grand setup, teachin' us how tae tend tae the earth and appreciate the food on our plates. Maggie Stewart, Duck Stewart's dochter from Loan Heath fairm, was the cook. She'd

ON AND OFF THE RAILS

work wonders wi' the produce we brought in, turnin' them intae hearty meals.

Mrs Munroe and Mrs Thomson dished oot the dinners. They were like a tag team in the canteen, keepin' things runnin' smoothly and makin' sure we a' got fed. The only bad day was Friday—prunes and custard. I hated prunes. It was like tryin' tae swallow wee, wrinkled pieces o' shite. We had tae sit there until we ate them. I'd eat the custard and leave the prunes, hopin' tae escape their clutches.

Mrs Munroe would stand over me, arms crossed and a stern look on her face, sayin', "Ye'll fuckin' eat them, and ye're nae leavin' here till ye do!" I'd stare at the prunes, contemplatin' my fate, then reluctantly shovel them intae my mouth while she watched. We had a good laugh about it later, though at the time it felt like torture.

The garden classes were more than just a lesson in horticulture; they were a lesson in life. We learned patience as we waited for the seeds tae sprout, responsibility as we tended tae the plants, and the value o' hard work when we harvested our crops. The sense o' pride we felt when we saw our veggies bein' served in the canteen was immense. It made the hard work worth it, knowin' we were contributin' tae somethin' bigger than ourselves.

The camaraderie in the garden was somethin' special too. We'd work side by side, chattin' and laughin', sometimes even singin' tae pass the time. It was a break from the usual classroom routine, and we relished every moment. The garden became a place o' peace and productivity, where we could escape the rigours o' academic life and get our hands dirty.

Maggie Stewart, with her fiery red hair and quick wit, became a beloved figure in the canteen. She'd often share stories about her days on the fairm, and we'd listen intently, imaginin' life on Loan Heath. Her meals were legendary, always full o' flavour and made wi' love. Even on prune and custard days, we knew we were lucky tae have such a dedicated cook.

Mrs Munroe and Mrs Thomson, despite their tough exteriors, had hearts o' gold. They cared

ON AND OFF THE RAILS

deeply for us kids and wanted tae make sure we were well-fed and looked after. Their no-nonsense approach in the canteen was balanced by moments o' kindness and humour. Lookin' back, I realise how much they shaped our school experience and how grateful I am for their presence.

Aye, those garden classes and the times in the canteen were some o' the best memories I have. They taught us more than just how tae grow vegetables—they taught us about community, hard work, and the simple joys o' life. Even the dreaded prunes have a place in those cherished memories, a reminder o' the lessons learned and the laughter shared.

Matlen Mackey, fa became the biggest ice cream maker in the west, used tae supply the school wi' milk. Every day, we'd get wee quarter-pint bottles, and it was a real treat. There was somethin' special aboot those bottles, the way the milk tasted so fresh and pure. Marty Thomson, fa sadly died a few years ago o' cancer, delivered the milk. He was a friendly chap, always had a smile and a kind word for us kids.

My favourite school meals were haggis, neeps, and tatties. There was nae better combination than that. We'd eat raw neeps, carrots, and tatties, especially efter a heavy frost. The neeps would be so solid ye could bounce them like a ball. We'd have a great time playin' wi' them before finally munchin' on them. The frost gave them a sweetness that made them irresistible.

But nae a' classes were fun. My least favourite were geography and history. A' that talk o' wars and who was fightin' who, it was a' a bit much for me. I couldnae see the point in learnin' aboot battles fought hundreds o' years ago. It felt so distant and irrelevant tae a young lad like me, more interested in the here and now.

Geography was another bore. A' those maps and places I'd never heard of, it didnae hold my interest. I'd much rather be oot in the fields, workin' wi' my hands, or drivin' the tractor. The classroom was restrictive, while the fairm offered freedom and

ON AND OFF THE RAILS

adventure. It was hard tae concentrate on lessons when my mind was wanderin' tae the tasks waitin' for me back home.

We'd sit in those classes, half-listenin' tae the teacher drone on, our minds elsewhere. I'd doodle in my jotter or stare oot the window, dreamin' o' the next adventure. Even the best teachers struggled tae make those subjects exciting. It was just the way o' it.

But despite my lack o' enthusiasm for those classes, I still managed tae get through them. It was a matter o' puttin' in the bare minimum tae pass and then focusin' on the things I really enjoyed. School was a mixed bag, but it was the friendships, the mischief, and the moments o' joy that made it worthwhile.

Aye, Matlen Mackey's milk deliveries, the haggis, neeps, and tatties, and the adventures wi' my pals, they a' made up for the dull classes. Those memories are what I hold on tae, and they brin' a smile tae my face even now.

WILLIAM SCATTERTY

Harvey Cotter, the big American fa sells bikes in Edinburgh and Glasgow noo, used tae repair bikes fae the dump. He was a sight tae see, carryin' ten or twelve bike frames slung ower his shoulders and twenty wheels strapped aroond him. Harvey made bikes in his fairm shed, and he was a genius wi' a wrench. He'd take auld, battered frames and turn them intae gleamin' new bikes, ready for another adventure. I got a trike fae him for two bob—like ten pence today. Money's changed so much; it's ridiculous. Harvey's father was a cattleman, their hoose noo in ruins, but Harvey made a name for himsel' wi' his bikes.

My trike had iron wheels and a slidin' boot, a right mess o' red and blue paint. It wasnae much tae look at, but it was mine, and I loved it. I remember wreckin' my sister's bike once, crashin' intae a fence and landin' in the coos' bath. Mum and Dad laughed, but my sister was fumin'. She chased me roond the fairm wi' a broom, threatenin' tae knock me intae next week. We had cyclin' proficiency tests, but someone dismantled my sister's back

ON AND OFF THE RAILS

brake. I crashed intae a fence again, wreckin' her bike for the second time. I got a hidin' fae the bobby and Dad for that one. The bobby twasted my ear while Dad gave me a boot up the backside. It was a right lesson in lookin' efter things properly.

We had some fights at school, but it was a' in good fun. We'd scrabble and wrestle, usually endin' wi' a handshake and a laugh. There was nae malice in it, just the rough and tumble o' growin' up. Even the teachers understood it was part o' bein' a lad. They'd scold us, but there was a twinkle in their eye. They kent we were just lettin' off steam.

Harvey Cotter's bikes were legendary. He'd get requests fae a' ower, folk wantin' him tae fix up their auld bikes or make somethin' special for their kids. He had a knack for takin' junk and turnin' it intae treasure. His fairm shed was a wonderland o' parts and tools, and we'd spend hours there, watchin' him work his magic. Harvey wasnae just a bike repairman; he was a storyteller, regalin' us wi' tales o' his adventures and the history o' each bike he worked on. Every scratch and dent had a story, and Harvey kent them a'.

I was bullied for a while, but I had a couple o' lads who stuck up for me. The bullies, a pair o' bastards, would knock us aboot and steal our marbles. We used steel ball bearings from tractor wheels for marbles. They were heavier than the glass ones and could knock anythin' oot o' the ring. One o' the bullies is in charge o' the kids' fairm at Huntly now. Canae sue the truth, eh? It's funny how things turn oot.

Gettin' beaten was part o' school life. If ye stepped oot o' line, ye got whalloped. It was alright in winter—yer hands were freezin', so a slap wi' the belt warmed them up. Ye'd stand there, hands out, waitin' for the sting. It was a strange kind o' comfort. We never used our pen knives for anythin' but parin' pencils. They were tools, nae weapons. Nowadays, kids stab teachers. What's that aboot? I saw a nine-year-auld wi' a machete for protection. In my day, a fight ended when a kid was knocked

ON AND OFF THE RAILS

doon, and ye were friends by the end o' the day. Ye'd shake hands, dust yersel' aff, and get on wi' it.

The bullies back then were a real pain in the arse, though. They'd ambush us on the way hame, grabbin' our bags and tossin' our books in the muck. But I had a couple o' good mates, tough lads who wouldnae stand for any shite. They'd step in, and before ye knew it, we'd be scrapin' in the mud, rollin' aboot like a bunch o' wildcats. It was rough, but it taught ye tae stand up for yersel'.

We used tae play marbles wi' those steel ball bearings, and the bullies hated it when we beat them at their ain game. They'd try tae take them, but we'd hide the best ones in our socks. Ye could hear them clinkin' as we walked. It was a badge o' honour tae have the best marbles, and we guarded them wi' oor lives.

Lookin' back, it's amazin' how different things are noo. Back then, respect was instilled wi' a swift clip roond the ear. Ye kent where ye stood, and so did the teachers. They had nae time for nonsense. If ye acted up, ye paid the price. It was a tough love approach, but it worked. Ye learned quick and grew up even quicker.

The world's changed a lot since those days. Kids today, they've got a different kind o' toughness, but sometimes I think they've missed oot on the lessons we learned. There's nae respect like there used tae be. A fight then was a way tae settle differences, but it ended wi' a handshake and a sense o' mutual respect. Now, it's a different story. But those memories, they stay wi' ye, remindin' ye o' a time when life was simpler, even if it was a bit rough aroond the edges.

I once smashed a school window and had to pay for it. If ye did damage, ye paid for it. Simple as that. We got thrown oot o' school once for blowin' up a science class. The headmaster left us tae mix oor ain chemicals. We didna ken what we were doin', and the mixture started bubblin'. There was a loud bang, and we blew the window oot. The fire brigade and police came. The headmaster got knocked ower by the door when he came back. We jumped oot the window and got taken away by the fire

ON AND OFF THE RAILS

brigade. We learned no' tae mix chemicals after that!

It was quite the scene. We were just a bunch o' curious kids, messin' aroond in the science lab, thinkin' we were proper scientists. We'd seen experiments in books and thought, "How hard can it be?" So we started mixin' everythin' we could find—sulphur, saltpetre, some other stuff we couldnae even pronounce. We had no idea what we were doin', but it was excitin'.

The mixture started fizzin' and bubblin' like some kind o' witch's brew. We were standin' there, eyes wide, watchin' it go. Then, all o' a sudden, there was a massive bang. The whole room shook, and the windows blew oot, glass flyin' everywhere. Smoke filled the room, and the smell—oh, it was somethin' fierce.

The next thing we ken, the fire alarm's blarin', and folk are runnin' aboot like headless chickens. The headmaster came stormin' back in, but the door flew open wi' such force it knocked him flat on his arse. We didnae wait tae see what he'd do next.

We legged it oot the window, coughin' and splutterin', and landed in a heap on the grass outside.

The fire brigade arrived in no time, hoses at the ready, lookin' like they'd just landed in the middle o' a war zone. They rounded us up and checked we were alright before givin' us a right bollockin'. The polis showed up too, lookin' more amused than angry, which was a small mercy. They took statements, and we tried tae explain we were just tryin' tae learn. They didnae seem tae buy it, but they didnae arrest us either.

The headmaster was fumin'. He stood there, covered in soot and lookin' like he was ready tae explode himself. "Ye made us look like a bunch o' eejits!" he roared. "What the hell were ye thinkin'?" We didnae have much o' an answer, just stood there shufflin' oor feet and tryin' no' tae laugh.

After that, the headmaster made sure we never mixed chemicals unsupervised again. We got a proper lecture on safety, and the science lab was out o' bounds for a while. It was a hard lesson, but one we never forgot. Oor curiosity had nearly cost us oor necks, but it also gave us a story we'd tell for years. Every time we passed that broken window, we'd smirk and remember the day we nearly blew up the school.

School was different back then. Nae security, nae computers. We did everythin' in oor heids or wrote it oot. When I visited ma auld school recently, I was shocked at all the security. Metal detectors, security guards—it's a Scottish school in the middle o' nowhere! Back in ma day, we'd wander through the woods without a care. On ma visit, I ended up arguin' wi' a bloke who'd put a fence through the woods. "That fence is a right o' way, ye fuckin' wanker!" I shouted. We had a good row until his boss, who knew me, came along and cleared things up.

Schools now have metal detectors and security guards. Kids as young as four or five face this. Back in ma day, we had blackboards and chalk. It took me eighteen months to learn a mobile phone. Ma nine-year-auld nephew had to show me how. I prefer the auld ways.

Drumblade school was full o' characters and chaos, but it was ours. We had great fun, and it's a wonder we survived it all. But survive we did, and those days left a lastin' mark on us all.

I mean, think aboot it. In ma day, we didnae have the luxury o' instant answers at oor fingertips. If ye wanted to ken somethin', ye had to either remember it, look it up in a book, or ask somebody who knew. It made ye use yer brain more, made ye think. And that walk tae school, five miles each way, come rain, sleet, or snow—ye didnae see us complainin'. We were hardy kids, resilient tae the core.

The woods we wandered through were like a second home tae us. We knew every tree, every path, every hidden nook where ye could find a bit o' peace or get up tae mischief. We played games, built forts, and pretended tae be explorers in those woods. They were our playground, our classroom, and our sanctuary. We learned so much just by

ON AND OFF THE RAILS

bein' outdoors, far more than we ever did sittin' in a classroom.

So, ye can imagine ma surprise when I visited Drumblade recently and saw that fence. It cut right through the heart o' the woods, blockin' off paths we'd used for years. I couldnae believe it. That's why I gave the bloke a piece o' ma mind. "That fence is a right o' way, ye fuckin' wanker!" I shouted. He looked at me like I'd lost ma mind, but I wasnae havin' it. Luckily, his boss came along, and he knew me. He sorted it oot, and we had a good laugh aboot the old days.

It's no' just the security that's changed. The whole feel o' school is different now. The kids, they're glued tae screens, always tappin' away on their phones or tablets. Back then, we had blackboards and chalk, and if the teacher caught ye daydreamin', ye'd get a bit o' chalk lobbed at yer heid. And dinnae get me started on mobile phones. It took me eighteen months tae figure oot how tae use mine. Ma nine-year-auld nephew had tae show me how! I miss the simplicity o' the auld ways.

54

WILLIAM SCATTERTY

Drumblade school was a place full o' life and laughter. Sure, it was chaotic, and we got up tae all sorts o' trouble, but it was ours. The teachers, like Mrs Steven, were strict but fair. They didnae put up wi' any nonsense, but they also cared aboot us. They wanted us tae learn, tae grow, and tae be the best we could be.

The friendships we formed back then were strong and true. We looked oot for each other, stood up tae bullies, and shared in each other's joys and sorrows. Those experiences, those lessons learned, have stayed wi' me all ma life. They shaped who I am, and for that, I'm grateful.

Aye, Drumblade was a place o' characters and chaos, but it was also a place o' heart and soul. We had great fun, and it's a wonder we survived it all. But survive we did, and those days left a lastin' mark on us all.

ON AND OFF THE RAILS

My sister anne and I

TAKEN

It started off like any other day. I went tae school, ma mind focused on the usual lessons and the familiar faces o' ma classmates. But around twelve o'clock, everythin' changed. Without warnin', someone came intae the classroom and spoke quietly tae the headmaster. He looked at me, a strange expression on his face, and asked me tae come oot tae the lobby. The sound o' the classroom door shuttin' behind me echoed ominously, and I felt a chill run doon ma spine.

Standin' in the lobby were two strangers, social workers I would later find oot, but in that moment, they were just unknown figures who seemed tae hold ma fate in their hands. They didnae offer any explanations. They simply took me by the arm and led me away. The headmaster, caught off guard, stood there, as confused as I was. He didnae say a word, just watched as I was escorted oot o' the school.

I was terrified. Ma heart pounded in ma chest, and ma mind raced wi' questions. Why was this happening? Where were they takin' me? The fear gripped me, makin' ma legs feel weak and ma throat dry. I glanced back, hopin' for some sign o' reassurance, but all I saw were the bewildered faces o' ma classmates and teachers, starin' at me through the windows, powerless tae dae onything.

The car ride felt like an eternity. The social workers tried tae make small talk, but I couldnae focus on their words. Ma thoughts were a whirlwind o' panic and confusion. When we finally arrived at the care home in Inverurie, the reality o' ma situation began tae sink in. I was far frae hame, surrounded by strangers, and the fear only intensified.

WILLIAM SCATTERTY

Everythin' felt surreal, like a bad dream I couldnae wake up from. The care home was cauld and unwelcoming, a stark contrast tae the warmth o' ma ain hame. The ither bairns looked at me wi' curiosity and pity, but I felt utterly alone. The sense o' abandonment and helplessness was overwhelming.

My mum didnae ken anythin' aboot it. She came stormin' intae the school like a whirlwind, her face a mask o' worry and rage. Mr McLeod, the headmaster, met her at the door. "Well, you've been told, havenae ye?" he said, tryin' tae keep his composure.

Mum's eyes flared wi' confusion and anger. "What the fuck are ye on aboot?" she demanded, her voice echoin' through the quiet corridors.

Mr McLeod hesitated, lookin' a bit flustered. "He's gone tae Inverurie. The social worker came and picked him up, took him away."

Mum's face turned ashen, her hands clenchin' at her sides. "On whose orders?" she shouted, her voice nearly breakin' wi' desperation. But Mr

ON AND OFF THE RAILS

McLeod couldnae give her an answer that made any sense. He was just as much in the dark as she was.

What I didnae ken was that three days later, she turned up at the social worker's office, nae alone but armed wi' my dad's shotgun. She was a tiny woman, only 5'3", but built like an engine, pure determination and fury. The shotgun was empty, nae bullets in it, but that didnae matter. She was there tae make a point, and if there had been bullets, I dinnae doubt for a second she would have used them.

She burst into the office, her voice thunderin' like a storm. "Where the hell is my bairn? Ye better start talkin' or so help me, I'll blast ye tae pieces!" The social workers were cowerin' behind their desks, pale as ghosts. Mum was like a force o' nature, and nobody, nae even the authorities, could stand in her way when it came tae her kids. She was the boss o' the house, and that was that. If anybody touched her bairns, god help them.

Her rage was palpable, a mix o' terror and maternal instinct. The social workers couldnae give her the answers she wanted, but they knew better than tae cross her again. Mum's protectiveness was legendary, and that day, it became the stuff o' local lore.

But back to the day I was taken, after my mum went to the school to find me, the social workers brought me back hame tae the fairm tae get my belongings. It was strange bein' back, but it wasnae a happy visit. They just told my mum they were takin' me tae a kids' home because she wasnae fit tae look after me.

My mum, that wee fierce woman, didnae take kindly tae bein' told she wasnae capable. She marched straight intae the hoose, came back wi' my dad's shotgun, and chased them oot. I've never seen two people run so fast in my life. Mum's face was red wi' fury, her eyes blazin' like fire.

"Ye think ye can just take my bairn awa' and tell me I'm no fit? Get oot o' here afore I blast ye!" she screamed, her voice echoin' across the fairm.

The social workers were pale as sheets, scramblin' tae get away. They dragged me intae the

ON AND OFF THE RAILS

car, their hands shakin', and sped off like bats oot o' hell. Mum stood there, firin' the shotgun over the top o' the car as they tore doon the road. The sound o' the shots ringin' oot behind us made my heart race, a mix o' fear and strange pride in my mum's protectiveness.

It was pure chaos, the scene etched in my mind forever. Naebody messed wi' my mum and got away wi' it. She was a force o' nature, and that day, she showed them just how far she'd go tae protect her own. As the car sped awa', I could still see her standin' there, defiant, the shotgun still smokin' in her hands. I felt a mix o' pride and terror, knowin' that even though she couldnae stop them, she made damn sure they knew they were nae welcome.

The drive tae Inverurie seemed endless. My mind raced wi' fear and uncertainty. Whit kind o' place were they takin' me tae? Whit kind o' people would be there? Nae more familiar faces, nae more fairm, nae more mum tae stand up for me. Just the unknown, loomin' ahead like a dark, forebodin' storm. I tried tae hold back the tears, but it was nae use. The fear o' whit was tae come, and the loss o' whit I was leavin' behind, weighed heavy on my young heart.

CARE HOME FROM HELL

I arrived at the care home aroond four in the afternoon. The place was run by Bert and Daisy, and it was a hellhole. I spent two years there, losin' precious time o' my youth. I was taken awa' fae my mum at thirteen, in 1965, because I kept shittin' masel'. They nivver understood that my paralysed bowel was the cause o' my issues, which was yet tae be discovered as the root o' my troubles.

When I arrived, Daisy was there, but Bert himsel' didnae come hame until later. He was a top councillor and a nasty bastard. He didnae like me, and I didnae like him. He said I was mouthy, kent too much, and a' the rest o' it. I often telt him I'd tak

ON AND OFF THE RAILS

him oot tae the gairden and kick him aboot, but he wouldnae come outside wi' me.

The care home was an ordinary hoose wi' four bedrooms—lasses on the bottom floor, lads on the top. The air felt heavy wi' despair, and the walls seemed tae close in aroond me. Every day was a struggle tae keep my head abune water. The routine was brutal—early mornings, hard chores, and constant surveillance. Meals were sparse and tasteless, and the atmosphere was thick wi' fear and anger.

The other kids and I formed a bond, united by oor shared suffering. We'd whisper tae each other at night, sharin' oor dreams o' escape and better days. It was the only comfort we had in that dark place. I missed my family terribly and felt like a stranger in this cauld, unfeelin' place.

Bert was especially cruel, takin' any chance he got tae belittle and punish us. He had a way o' makin' ye feel like ye were nae worth the dirt under his shoes. Daisy was nae better, turnin' a blind eye tae his abuses and addin' her own brand o' cruelty.

WILLIAM SCATTERTY

As much as I despised Bert and Daisy, the other kids and I found small ways tae rebel, tae hold on tae a sense o' ourselves. We'd sneak oot at night, slidin' doon the drainpipe and runnin' off into the dark. Those brief moments o' freedom were like breaths o' fresh air in a suffocatin' world.

The thought o' endurin' this place for any length o' time filled me wi' dread. I longed for the day I could escape, return tae my family, and leave this nightmare behind. Each day, I wondered how I'd ever make it through. The constant ache o' missin' my mum and the familiar comforts o' home was almost unbearable.

It was clear from the start that I wasnae welcome there. Every day was a battle, and I often found masel' thinkin' back tae the warmth o' the fairm, the sound o' my mum's voice, and the simple joys o' my previous life. Those memories kept me going, givin' me strength tae face another day in that godforsaken place.

The care home was an ordinary hoose wi' four bedrooms—lasses on the bottom floor, lads on the

ON AND OFF THE RAILS

top. It had a worn facade, the paint peelin' aff the windowsills, and a door that creaked somethin' fierce every time it opened. The air inside always had a faint smell o' bleach and old carpets, a stark reminder o' its institutional nature.

Among the residents was a full family frae Ireland, the Monaghans frae County Antrim. There was Davey Monaghan, a braw lad who went on tae play for the Rangers and Celtic in Aberdeen. He was a legend in his ain right, wi' stories about his football exploits keepin' us entertained for hours. His brother, Peter, started as a council mechanic and worked his way up tae manager. He was clever wi' his hands, always tinkerin' wi' something. Brenda was a care assistant, kind-hearted but wi' her own troubles. Carol, a nurse, had a touch that was surprisingly gentle in a place so harsh. John, the brave soul, joined the army and met his end in a tragic hit-and-run. Then there was Katie, who had nine bairns tae nine different blokes, startin' when she was just thirteen. Her life was a whirlwind o' chaos and heartache.

WILLIAM SCATTERTY

Peter had a unique talent—he could mimic a budgie perfectly. We'd laugh until our sides hurt listenin' tae his uncanny impersonations. Years later, it was heartbreakin' when he was found dead in his hoose, three days before the police kicked the door open and discovered him.

Mary, another resident, was known for havin' nine bairns by nine different blokes. Her story was a stark reminder o' the struggles many faced. Amidst it all, there was Davey, the famous footballer who played for Celtic, Rangers, and some big teams in England. His tales were like a breath o' fresh air in an otherwase stiflin' environment.

Despite the bleak surroundings, I found companionship in Peter, Brenda, Carol, and John. They were my mates, my lifeline in that dark place. We bonded over our shared miseries and small victories. The emotional toll was heavy, but we clung tae each other for support. The memories o' those times are etched in my mind—the whispered conversations after lights out, the secret plans tae

ON AND OFF THE RAILS

escape, and the rare moments o' laughter that broke through the gloom.

Every day was a battle, but those friendships made the struggle bearable. The house itself might have been a hellhole, but the people, for all their flaws and scars, brought a flicker o' hope and humanity into the darkest corners o' our lives.

When I arrived at the home, they scrubbed me with a scrubbin' brush, as if I was nae more than dirt they needed to scrape aff the floor. The bristles dug into my skin, leavin' it raw and red. They were nasty bastards, each one more heartless than the last. That hoose has since been knocked down and rebuilt, but the memories are as vivid as ever. I've never been back, but I want to. I want to go back and confront the ghosts o' my past. I want it shut down, the very ground it stands on salted so nothin' can grow there again. When I go to court, I'll ask the judge to close it for good. Kids dinnae deserve that. They're still bein' abused to this day, and it needs to end.

WILLIAM SCATTERTY

The housekeeper was a real piece o' work. She used to hit us with shovels and all sorts. I canae even remember her name now, but she's dead and gone, thank God. The abuse and mistreatment were rampant, like a plague that infected everyone who lived and worked there. It's why there's a Historic Child Abuse court bein' held now. I'm hopin' for justice, finally. I've still got an unopened report from that time, a tangible reminder o' the horrors I endured. I want tae see those bastards pay for what they did, for the years they stole from me and so many others.

They started beatin' me as soon as I got there. The bruises barely had time to form before I got another walloping. The social worker was no better. He beat the shite out o' me and my two mates. Every slap, punch, and kick was meant to break us, but it just made me more determined to fight back.

The housekeeper was a real nasty bastard. Her eyes always seemed to gleam with a sick delight whenever she had a chance to hurt us. One day, I'd had enough. When she came at me with her usual

ON AND OFF THE RAILS

viciousness, I whacked her across the face with a shovel. I remember the satisfyin' crunch as her nose broke, her eyes blackened, and four o' her teeth went flying. Daisy was alright, but his wife, she was a right piece o' work. And can ye believe it, Bert was a county councillor! The very people meant to protect us were the ones dishin' out the most pain. It was a hellish place, run by monsters masqueradin' as caretakers.

The only decent soul in that hellhole was Charlie, the gardener. He seemed tae care, or at least he didnae join in wi' the rest o' them. But decent folk were few and far between in that place. One time, the district nurse gave me an enema, and when I accidentally got her wet, she whalloped me good and proper. My guts were sore for days after that.

They didnae like me, nae at all, because I told them exactly whit I thought. I didnae care aboot the consequences; I just couldnae keep my mouth shut. It was my way o' fightin' back, even if it meant mair beatings. I wasnae gonnae let them break me completely, nae matter how hard they tried.

WILLIAM SCATTERTY

Every day was the same brutal routine. We got beaten afore we even had a chance tae start the day. The care home director would belt us daily afore sendin' us tae class, makin' sure we were too broken tae think o' resistin'. The pain became a part o' our existence, just like breathin'.

I wouldnae go tae school, no if I could help it. We were only half an hour fae Inverurie Academy, but I preferred wanderin' aroond instead o' sittin' in a classroom. What was the point when every day started and ended wi' a beatin'? I hardly ever went tae school, but when I did, I tried tae make the most o' it. Despite everything, I managed tae sit my O-levels there and got three—English, Maths, and Metalwork and Woodwork. It felt like a small victory in a sea o' defeats, a reminder that even in the darkest places, there was still a glimmer o' hope.

Aye, I made a few bob at school by pinchin' matchbox toys fae the local toyshop and floggin' them. Ye wouldnae believe how much demand there was for those wee cars among the lads. Made

ON AND OFF THE RAILS

aboot twa quid a day, which was a fortune tae a school lad like me. I felt like a right entrepreneur, sneakin' intae the shop, slippin' the toys intae my pockets, and sellin' them aff in the playground. We had our own black market goin' on.

One day, I was feelin' extra confident, thinkin' I was untouchable. I strolled intae the shop, noddin' tae the shopkeeper like I was just another innocent bairn lookin' around. I grabbed a few matchbox cars, the shiny ones that all the lads wanted, and slipped them intae my jacket. Just as I was makin' my way oot, the shop bloke, a grumpy auld man wi' thick glasses and a baldy heid, grabbed me by the scruff o' the neck.

"Turn oot yer pockets, ye wee thief!" he snarled, his face red wi' rage.

I tried tae keep ma cool, but my heart was poundin'. I slowly turned oot my pockets, and the cars tumbled oot, clatterin' tae the floor. He looked at me, eyes wide wi' disbelief, and I mustered up the cheekiest grin I could manage.

WILLIAM SCATTERTY

"I dinna ken how they got there," I said, tryin' tae sound innocent. "They must have fallen aff the shelf while I was walkin' past!"

The audacity o' it, but that was me, always tryin' tae wriggle oot o' trouble. The man was fumin', his face turnin' an even deeper shade o' red. He grabbed me by the ear and marched me oot the shop, mutterin' curses under his breath.

"Oot ye go, and dinna come back!" he roared, practically throwin' me oot the door.

As soon as I was oot, I ran like the wind, my heart racin' but laughin' tae masel'. The lads at school were in stitches when I told them the tale, and I had tae admit, it was worth it for the laugh. I kept my distance fae that shop for a while, but it didnae stop me fae findin' other ways tae make a few bob. Ye learn tae be resourceful when ye grow up in a place like that.

Aye, overall, I really hated it. The place was pure hell. I used to see my mum two or three times a week, and those were the only moments o' light in that dark time. Peter, John, and I were inseparable,

ON AND OFF THE RAILS

always schemin' tae get away fae that place. We sometimes walked fae Donworth to Edinburgh tae John's auntie's. She was a kind woman, always ready wi' a hot meal for us. She'd feed us, let us rest for a bit, then she'd call the bobbies tae take us back. We knew it was comin', but we were grateful for the brief respite.

The police were alright—they never abused us, just did their job. They'd pick us up, maybe shake their heids a bit, but they'd always get us back safely. The real trouble started when the school would phone the home and tell them we'd been skippin'. That's when the beltings would come.

I remember one time, clear as day, my head was banged aff three walls in the livin' room. The sheer force o' it made my ears ring, and for a moment, everythin' went black. It was a brutal place, and it left scars on all o' us. The physical pain was one thing, but the constant fear, the anxiety o' knowin' that any small misstep would lead to another beating, that was the real torment.

WILLIAM SCATTERTY

Peter, John, and I found comfort in each other's company. We were like brothers, united against the common enemy. We shared our dreams o' escape, whispered plans late at night, and clung to the hope that one day we'd be free o' that place.

We snuck awa fae the home every night, wanderin' doon tae Edinburgh, Glasgow, Leeds, an' Inverness. We'd gae tae bed at seven o'clock, but by half past nine, we were oot that windae, slidin' doon the drainpipe, an' aff intae the night. We'd run doon the road laughin', feelin' the thrill o' freedom, even if it was jist for a few hours. We had great fun, great adventures. We'd try tae catch the night wagon tae Aberdeen. Some drivers let us on, but we'd jump the trailers an' hide under the cupboards. The polis would pick us up, take us back tae the station, gie us a bite tae eat, an' ask whit we were daein' wanderin' the streets.

The social workers, if she came tae pick us up, would knock the livin' shit oot o' us in the back o' the car. She was a right nasty piece o' work. Imagine that, she retired an' became a Labour MP. How

ON AND OFF THE RAILS

does that work? Ye tell me! The whole thing's a farce if ye ask me.

Those nightly escapades were our only escape fae the misery o' the care home. We'd feel the cauld air on our faces, see the lights o' the city in the distance, an' for a wee while, we could pretend we were free. It was a grand adventure, even if it always ended wi' a rough return tae reality. The fear o' gettin' caught was always there, but it was worth it for those few precious hours o' freedom. We'd laugh, run, an' explore the countryside, dreamin' o' a better life, far fae the beatings an' cruelty we faced daily.

In the end, it was those moments o' rebellion that kept us sane. They gave us a taste o' freedom, a reminder that there was a world beyond the walls o' the care home. It was a harsh life, but we faced it the best we could, findin' joy an' camaraderie in our small acts o' defiance. Those nights on the run, they were the only times we truly felt alive.

On oor final adventure, somethin' different happened. After the polis picked us up, they saw the pain we were in and decided tae get a doctor tae look at us. I was black an' blue, covered in bruises frae head tae toe. The doctor, a stern-lookin' man wi' kind eyes, stripped us doon. I resisted at first, but he was insistent. He cut ma shirt aff, revealin' the full extent o' the bruises. I wouldnaetell him what happened, but somehow, he kent. His face hardened wi' anger an' determination.

He wasted nae time. He got an ambulance tae take us tae the hospital. I can still remember the siren's wail as we sped through the streets, feelin' a mix o' fear an' relief. It was the first time that someone outside the care home seemed tae care aboot what was happenin' tae us. We spent four days in that hospital, under the watchful eyes o' nurses an' doctors who treated us wi' kindness. They asked questions, but I kept ma mouth shut. Still, the medical staff had seen enough. They kent we were bein' abused.

Efter that, I was transferred tae a mental hospital. The place was cold an' clinical, a stark contrast tae the chaotic hellhole I'd been livin' in. It was nae better, but it was different. The staff there had their own ways o' makin' life miserable, but at least the constant physical beatings were over.

Bein' taken awa frae ma mum an' put in that care hame was the worst time o' ma life. I lost twa years in that hellhole, years I cannae get back. I want justice for what they did tae me. I hope Judge Donaldson sends those bastards tae prison. And when I die, I'm gaun tae haunt them a'. They'll be sorry they ever messed wi' me.

I'll nae let them forget what they did. Every bruise, every scar, every sleepless night—they'll pay for it. They thought they could break me, but here I am, still standin', still fightin'. Naebody deserves tae go through what we did. I'm speakin' up for a' the bairns who suffered, a' the wee souls who didna make it.

When I stand in court, I'll look those bastards in the eye an' tell them, "Ye didna break me. Ye tried, but ye failed." And when they're locked up, they'll ken it was me who put them there. And if justice isnae served in this life, I'll make sure it's served in the next. Aye, they'll be sorry they ever crossed paths wi' me.

BEHIND LOCKED DOORS

Life in the mental hospital was nae walk in the park, but it was a shift frae the relentless abuse o' the care home. It was a new kind o' nightmare, one where I had tae fight tae keep ma sanity intact. I'd lost two years tae that care home, an' now I was facin' another kind o' prison. But I was determined nae tae let them beat me. I'd come this far, an' I wasnae gaun tae give up now.

Now, I shouldnae hae been in there; it was against the law. I was only fourteen for fuck's sake. Ye could only be put in there wi' a court order or by the polis, but ye had tae be eighteen-plus. I was four years under that.

ON AND OFF THE RAILS

I was in there for three months. It was fuckin' awful. I was in a locked ward wi' mental cases. One or two o' them were nae too bad. The nicht nurses an' the day nurses were nae too bad. Bill Staten, Fraser, Jimmy Riddle, an' Big Henry were some o' the nurses. They looked efter us well, got tae gie them their due. The ward overlooked the grounds an' the main road. I used tae watch Henry an' Jimmy Riddle gaun hame in the mornin'. Jimmy had a minivan an' Henry had a Cortina. A nicer bloke ye couldnae hae met.

Bein' stuck in the mental ward was pure hell. It was a locked ward, ken. Every time I needed tae gae tae the bathroom, they had tae unlock the door. It was a right palaver. They wouldnae lock the toilet door itself, but they'd lock ye intae the ward. So if ye needed back in, ye had tae knock on the door like some kind o' prisoner. I could hae legged it, but I didnae ken where tae gae. I kent I was in Cornhill village, but bein' a country boy, I couldnae get used tae that. The whole place felt alien tae me.

WILLIAM SCATTERTY

The ward was constantly filled wi' the noise o' doors clankin' and folk mutterin' tae themselves. The air had a strange smell, like disinfectant mixed wi' despair. I'd lie awake at night, listenin' tae the distant sounds o' the outside world – a dog barking, the occasional car passin' by – and dream o' the open fields back hame. The confines o' that place made me feel like a caged animal, and I longed for the freedom tae just wander the countryside, free as a bird.

Cornhill village might hae been jist doon the road, but it may as well hae been on another planet. I missed the smell o' fresh-cut hay, the sight o' the hills in the distance, and the feel o' the wind on my face. Inside that ward, everythin' was suffocating.

I was the only young person in the mental hospital. The rest were in their 40s and 50s. I saw dead bodies! There was a screen thing alang the bed, but ye'd still see them put the poor fella intae the zinc trolley. When ye heard that trolley comin', ye kent someone was dead. It had four wheels and was shaped like a coffin. They'd put the body intae

ON AND OFF THE RAILS

that and wheel it away tae the undertakers. A good few died while I was there, mostly frae auld age and heart attacks.

There was this one bloke, 6'7" and built like a brick shithoose. It took ten nurses tae hold him down. They used tae give us paraldehyde. It paralysed us aw doon one side. They'd gie him 20ccs o' that stuff, and he'd be oot like a light for hours, half the day and night. He'd wake up calm, but somethin' would set him off a few days later, and he'd start his rampage again. Fuck me, tryin' tae hold him down was pure chaos. They'd sit on him and everything. It was a nightmare tae see for a fourteen-year-old, I tell ye.

The hospital ward was a grim place. The constant shufflin' o' feet, the clinkin' o' medical tools, and the groans and mutterings o' the patients created a hauntin' symphony. I remember the eerie silence that would follow the sound o' the trolley's wheels – a silence that seemed tae seep intae yer bones. The sight o' the dead bein' wheeled away, the stark reality o' it, was somethin' that stuck wi' me. It was a harsh reminder o' the fragility o' life, especially for someone so young.

That big bloke, the one built like a tank, was a force o' nature when he lost it. Ye could see the fear in the nurses' eyes every time he started tae stir. The paraldehyde they gave us was meant tae keep us calm, but it came wi' its ain set o' horrors. The feelin' o' bein' partially paralysed, unable tae move or speak properly, was terrifying. Ye'd be trapped in yer ain body, watchin' the madness unfold around ye. It was a livin' nightmare, and I often wondered if I'd ever escape it.

We'd get up at 7:30 in the mornin'. They'd come in wi' a trolley wi' yer breakfast. The porridge was lumpy as fuck, but the bacon and eggs were alright. Jeannie, the physiotherapist, was nice. She was an older lady, probably dead and gone by now.

The mornings started wi' a clang as the trolley rattled through the ward, wakin' us up. The porridge, lumpy and unappetisin', was a far cry frae the warm, smooth porridge my mum used tae make back home. Still, the bacon and eggs were a small comfort in an otherwase bleak routine. Jeannie, bless her, was a ray o' sunshine. She had a kind word for everyone, her gentle touch and warm smile made the physio sessions bearable. She'd chat away, askin' how we were, always tryin' tae make us feel better, even if just for a moment. Her presence was a reminder that there were still good people in the world.

I couldnae see any family members while I was in the mental hospital, not even my mum, whether she was in the care home or the hospital. That isolation was brutal. It felt like I'd been cut off frae the world, left tae fend for maself in this place where kindness was a rare commodity. I didnae handle it very well, if I'm bein' honest.

Every day was a struggle. The isolation, the strange faces, the regimented routine – it wasnae what I was used to. I missed the familiar faces, the comfort o' home, even the simple things like my mum's cookin' or the warmth o' our fairm. It was hard to keep going, tae find a reason tae get up every mornin'. The only thing that kept me sane was the thought o' gettin' out o' there one day.

Nae seein' my family took its toll on me. I felt like a prisoner, locked away frae the ones I loved. I'd lie awake at night, thinkin' o' my mum, wonderin' if she was alright, if she missed me as much as I missed her. It was a dark time, and there were moments when I thought I'd never see the outside world again. But somewhere deep inside, there was a flicker o' hope that kept me goin'.

There was no therapy in the hospital, just a lot o' aggression. I wasnae involved, but there was a lot o' violence towards the nurses. One doctor, in particular, didnae like me at all. We had many run-ins. I pinned him tae the wall by the throat one day because he pissed me off so much. I said, "Why dinnae ye fuck off and leave me alane? I'm only a kid, for God's sake!"

He said, "Ye assaulted me."

I replied, "I'll fuckin' kill you, never mind assault you, ye bastard." I completely lost my rag with him. It was the first time I lost my temper.

ON AND OFF THE RAILS

Since then, I've lost my temper a lot, especially durin' my time as a train driver. The doctor in the hospital would come along while we were moppin' the floor or daein'some other task, and he'd say things like, "Oh, ye missed a bit here, you're not very good at this," and so on. I took this for weeks until it finally boiled over.

One day, I picked up the bucket o' water and threw it over him. I put the bucket on his head and whacked him with the mop. I said, "Now fuckin' leave me alone or next time I'll shove this mop so far up yer arse it'll clean yer teeth!" That was another time I lost my temper. None o' the nurses did anything; they just stood there. Some o' them were laughin' about it because they were waitin' to see who would snap at him. He was drivin' people to the end o' their tether.

There was a lad in there who used to have six nurses hold him down. One day, he got hold o' the doctor and threw him through the window. It was a great plate glass window, about six feet tall, double glazed. He just picked him up and threw him through the window. The doctor landed in the field outside the ward and was taken away to the hospital in an ambulance to be looked at. The police and everythin' turned up. After that, he left me alone. He wouldnae come near me. He used to put me in the solitary unit for three or four days to calm me down. They'd give me a couple o' injections, and I'd sleep for a couple o' days. I was alright after that, but he never came near me again. He stayed well away from me.

The other doctor came around, and he was alright. I had nae problem with him. I just said, "Dinnae let that bastard near me. I'll kill the cunt if he comes near me."

He said, "I know ye dinnae like him."

I said, "Dinnae like him? I fuckin' hate the bastard."

The doctor said, "Okay, he will nae come near ye again."

They gave me the injection, and that's the last thing I remember for two days. They fed me by tube

ON AND OFF THE RAILS

down my throat to keep me going. When I woke up, I took the tube out and asked, "What was that for?"

They said, "Well, we had to feed you; you've been out cold."

I said, "That's alright then."

Overall, bein' in that mental hospital was a hellish experience. The constant violence, the lack o' therapy, and the oppressive atmosphere made it unbearable. But the worst was that doctor who drove everyone mad. I'm just glad I managed to get out o' there with my sanity somewhat intact.

Eventually, I went for a psychiatric test. They sat me down in an office wi' six papers. The psychiatrist said, "I'm gaun tae another room. I'll be back when ye finish them." So I did all the papers, put them back on the table, and just sat there, waiting. He came back in, went through all the papers, and he couldnaemake sense o' it.

He said, "What the hell are ye daein' here?" I said, "Well, ye tell me!" He says, "There's nothin' wrang wi' yer brain. Ye've got one, and ye ken how tae use it." I said, "Aye, well, I ken that, ye ken that, but those other bastards don't."

So, he referred me to the doctor. He said, "Look, there's nothin' wrang wi' this lad mentally. It's just his physical side; I think there's somethin' wrang." That's why he got me intae the hospital for an X-ray, and that's when they found the paralysed bowel. I spent my 15th birthday on the fuckin' operatin' table.

When the doctor did the tests, he said, "Pack yer suitcase, ye willnae be back."

He picked me up at six o'clock, and I said, "What do ye mean?"

He said, "Ye willnae be back, let's put it that way. This is nae place for you." He was adamant about that.

He came tae see me after the operation before he left and said, "How are ye feelin'?"

I said, "Well, a bit fuckin' rough, like."

He was in touch wi' my mum and said, "He'll be back wi' ye shortly."

ON AND OFF THE RAILS

After my operation, they put me in a halfway house for aboot three weeks, and then I was sent back tae my mum and dad.

Leavin' that place was like comin' oot o' a nightmare. I'd spent three months in that hellhole, surrounded by dead bodies and madness. But the operation gave me a second chance, a way tae start again. Bein' back wi' my family was a blessing, even wi' all the hardships. I knew I'd nae forget what happened in there, but I also knew I was stronger for havin' survived it. The bastards hadnae beaten me, and I was determined tae live my life on my ain terms, nae matter what.

THE OPERATIN' TABLE

And so, I had my fifteenth birthday on the operatin' table at Woodend Hospital. From there, I went tae a halfway house in Cots, and three weeks later, I went back tae my parents, back tae my Mum and Dad. I was born wi' a paralysed bowel, I was told afterwards. This doctor had me undergo psychiatric tests, and Mr Clark, the head psychiatrist at the time, said, "I dinnae know what the fuck you're daein' here. You've got nothin' wrang wi' yer head, just yer arse!" He said there's nothin' wrang wi' me mentally, it's the bottom half o' me that needs tae be seen to. The doctor said, "Six o'clock the mornin', I am takin' ye tae Woodend Hospital tae get a barium X-ray."

ON AND OFF THE RAILS

Noo, for a barium X-ray ye get a big jug o' milky water, it tastes fuckin' horrible, but it goes all through yer system. Ye have tae hold it inside ye for half an hour, then ye go and lie on the X-ray table, and they take a' the X-rays o' ye, frae yer head tae yer feet, tae find oot what's wrang wi' ye. They have all sorts o' computers and that now, but at that time, that's how they did yer X-ray. It took aboot three weeks for that stuff tae clear oot o' my body! At the end o' the day, this doctor and the surgeon had me on their X-ray table at 8 in the mornin', and then I was gettin' my surgery at 8am the followin' mornin'. I had nothin' tae eat and nothin' tae drink and had my 15th birthday on the operatin' table. I was oot for aboot 10 hours. He had tae open me up and take everythin' oot, my stomach and all, and lay it on the side. Then he put a steel plate intae my arse!

I'm the only bloke who has a special letter for when I go through the airports. When I go through, they have tae turn all the alarm systems off as the lights start flashin', the bells start ringin', and fuck knows what else. So I got a letter for the airport authority that they have tae switch everythin' off before I go through an airport now, and then they switch everythin' back on again. They have tae let me go through because I have a steel plate in my stomach. It's been in there for 57 years. I'm on tablets for the rest o' my life.

At 8:30 in the mornin', I was lyin' on the operatin' table, knocked oot. I was kept in the hospital for a week, then they put me intae a halfway house for three weeks, and then my dad came and picked me up and took me back tae Drumbeg. I was so glad tae come back home. Nothin' bad happened in the halfway house. It was alright; I was well-fed and all.

That halfway house was a mix o' people, but everybody left ye alone. It was me and Kenny, the two youngest. Kenny was in a wheelchair. I did three weeks in there then my dad came and collected me. Half o' them were in for something, there were prostitutes, so they were helpin' her wi' her life. Ye used tae get yer meals, a fiver a week

ON AND OFF THE RAILS

tae pay for yer meals. I was workin', so I could afford it. After I left, I was back on my feet.

A man and his wife ran the halfway house. She was the matron at Woodlands Hospital for disabled kids. That's why I started seein' the disabled kids and takin' them oot when I became a driver. We used tae hire minibuses from Mitchell's in Aberdeen, two or three. He asked one day what we were daein'wi' them, so we took him oot one day tae show what we were daein'wi' them, and he said from then on not tae pay for the minibuses. All we had tae do was pay for the petrol, we didnae pay for anythin' else.

I've had these health conditions follow me through my life. I took a heart attack when I was 14 years auld on Don Bridge in Inverurie. I was lookin' at the salmon jump, that's the last thing I remember. I woke up in a bed in the Aberdeen Royal Infirmary. I got a police escort in the ambulance, but I dinnae remember it. I got a pig's valve fitted; it's supposed tae be changed every ten years, but that's been in there since I was 14. It's

WILLIAM SCATTERTY

never been touched. I've had five heart attacks, four angina attacks. I should nae be here. They call me Wonderboy whenever I go tae the hospital, as they wonder why I'm still here! I say my mum doesnae want me up there, she runs the roost up there, her and my sister.

But back tae the halfway house. The man and his wife who ran it were decent folk, and they did their best tae make us feel human again. It was a far cry from the hellhole o' the care home and the madness o' the mental hospital. It was a place where I started tae heal, physically and mentally. I had a room tae maself, a warm bed, and three meals a day. Simple things that felt like luxuries after what I'd been through.

Kenny and I became fast friends. He was in a wheelchair, but he had a spirit that couldnae be broken. We'd sit up at night, talkin' about our dreams and what we'd do when we got out. Those conversations kept me going, gave me hope.

The day my dad came tae take me home was one o' the happiest days o' my life. We drove back tae

ON AND OFF THE RAILS

Drumbeg, the familiar sights and sounds o' the countryside fillin' me with a sense o' peace I hadnae felt in a long time. Walkin' back into our house, seein' my mum's face light up, it was like comin' back tae life.

Life has been a series o' battles, but I've come through them all. I've been cut open, stitched up, and sent back out into the world, but I'm still here. I've got a steel plate in my stomach, a pig's valve in my heart, and more scars than I care tae count, but I'm still standing. If there's one thing I've learned, it's that ye cannae let the bastards grind ye down. Ye've got tae stand up, fight back, and never, ever give up.

WILLIAM SCATTERTY

Mum, maself and sister Anne

LIFE ON THE RAILS

When I got back hame, I started my lifelong work on the rails! I got hame on a Friday and started on the railway on Monday. I was twenty-one when I first started driving. I was eighteen when I first started daein' a' the shunting. I only went for the interview as a promise tae my dad. I said I'd try it oot for three months and thought that would be that! But little did I ken it was tae become a lifelong love affair wi' the railways. I went for three months o' trainin' on the rails tae please my dad. I wasnae inspired by him, but my dad put me up for the job. The auld doc who did my medical check was half-cut, I swear. Reeked o' whisky and barely looked at the forms. He just squinted at me, gave a nod, and

ON AND OFF THE RAILS

stamped the paperwork. "You'll be fine, lad," he slurred. I walked out o' there half-wonderin' if I'd imagined it. But I passed, and that was that. He decided that as long as ye werenae colourblind, that was the most important thing on the railway. They wouldnae let ye in if ye were a criminal or colourblind. No point because ye need tae be able tae see red and green. I said I would do it for three months till somethin' else came up, and then I ended up daein'it for fifty years!

The first days on the railway were a mix o' excitement and nerves. The clatter o' the trains, the smell o' the diesel, and the constant movement— it was a world away from anythin' I'd known. My first tasks involved a lot o' heavy liftin' and manual labour, shuntin' the trains and makin' sure everythin' was in order. It was hard graft, but there was somethin' about the rhythm o' it that appealed to me.

The camaraderie among the railway men was somethin' special. We were a rough bunch, full o' banter and a bit rough around the edges, but there was a bond there. The railway yard was a place full o' noise and action, the constant clangin' o' metal, the hiss o' steam, and the shouts o' men directin' operations. I loved the feelin' o' bein' part o' somethin' so dynamic and essential.

Drivin' trains was a whole new world. When I got the chance tae start driving, it was like a dream come true. The power o' the engine beneath me, the tracks stretchin' out ahead—it was freedom like I'd never known. The first time I sat in the driver's seat, I felt a mix o' terror and exhilaration. There was a massive responsibility, knowin' that so many lives depended on ye daein' yer job right. But there was also a thrill, a sense o' control and mastery that was intoxicating.

I remember the first time I took control o' a train, my hands grippin' the controls, my heart poundin' in my chest. The world outside the cab blurred as we sped along the tracks. I had to concentrate, to feel the rhythm o' the train and the track, to know when to speed up and when to slow down. It was a

ON AND OFF THE RAILS

skill that came with time and experience, and I was determined to master it.

I grew tae love the railways, more than I ever thought possible. The sense o' purpose it gave me, the challenges it presented, and the comradeship o' my fellow workers made it more than just a job—it was a way o' life. The long hours, the hard work, and the responsibility were all part o' it. I took pride in every train I drove, every journey I completed.

The railway became my home. It gave me a sense o' belongin' that I had been searchin' for. Lookin' back, I can see that it wasnae just about drivin' trains; it was about findin' a place where I could be maself, where I could prove my worth. And I did. Every single day on those tracks, I proved it to maself and to everyone around me.

I started as a cleaner. Ye'd go in one end clean and come oot the other end completely black fae head tae toe. I had coal in my hair and everythin' else. Cleanin' the Black 5s was hard graft. The engines were massive, and every nook and cranny had tae be spotless. Ye'd come oot o' that job lookin' like a chimney sweep, covered in soot and grime. It was tough, dirty work, but it built character. Ye'd be scrubbin' away with yer brushes, gettin' into all the tight spots, makin' sure every inch o' that engine was gleaming. By the end o' the shift, ye could hardly recognise yerself.

Drivin' the diesels was a whole different ball game. The 24s, the 08 shunters, and the Class 14 "monkey" were powerful beasts. The Class 18, the 24, 25, 26, the 33 "Compton," and the 47s all had their quirks. Ye had tae learn tae handle each one, knowin' how they'd respond, their strengths and weaknesses. The whisky line was one o' my favourites. That auld diesel, ninety-three years old, was a rattlin' old thing, but it had character. Drivin' it fae Aberdeen tae Inverness and back was a rough ride, but there was a certain charm to it.

I can still remember the feelin' o' the controls in my hands, the power o' the engine beneath me. The thrill o' seein' the landscape whiz by, knowin' that I was in charge o' this massive machine. There was a sense o' freedom and responsibility that came with

ON AND OFF THE RAILS

it. The new trains, despite their fancy technology, never had the same soul as those old beasts.

I used to work at Gyle, which used tae be a big depot. There's fuck all there noo, just two platforms and that's it. There's council hooses where the yard used tae be. We had a big shed there, and that's where a' the steam engines were done, repaired, and cleaned. We used tae get up at three o'clock in the mornin', go rev the steam engine up, and get her goin' for five o'clock. We used tae do Gyle tae Inverness, then up tae Wick, then back tae Jordan Junction, up tae Sourdough, and back tae Jordan Junction, then back tae Inverness. Take a break, then back tae Gyle. Fourteen tae sixteen-hour days we had, seven days a week. Monday tae Sunday, a day aff, then back tae work on the Tuesday. We enjoyed it, though.

Some days I used tae go tae Inverness. Ye've got tae do the whiskey trail. The 107 is ninety-three years auld and still gaun strong. I used tae drive that thing frae Aberdeen tae Inverness and back. The 125s ye see doon in Edinburgh are the same ones I

WILLIAM SCATTERTY

used tae drive doon in Plymouth, Bea and Lyra, Ben Jance, and Temple Meads depot. That's where all those 125s up in Scotland come from now; they were all Great Western. They took all the auld engines oot—the V6 and V7 engines—and put in the V9, V10, and V11 engines for the hills in Scotland because the auld engines werenae strong enough tae get through the hills frae Pitlochry tae Inverness. Once ye're o'er the hill, ye're alright; ye could freewheel the thing tae Inverness as lang as ye got tae the top o' the hill.

We used tae have a steam engine breakfast! Ye got two shovels—a shorter shovel for yer breakfast, and a black shovel for yer coal. Ye put yer eggs, yer bacon, yer fried bread, and everythin' on the shovel, into the fire. Ten seconds, fifteen seconds, back oot, turn them o'er, put them back in the fire again for another ten seconds, brin' it back oot, and ye can sit there wi' yer eggs and bacon and yer mug o' tea. Ye kept that on top o' the fire tae keep it warm. That's how we used tae do it!

ON AND OFF THE RAILS

Those were the days when work was hard but honest. We worked lang hours, but there was a sense o' camaraderie that kept us gaun. The early mornings, the smell o' the steam, and the sound o' the engines roarin' tae life—it was magic. The sheds at Gyle were always bustlin' wi' activity, engines comin' in for repairs and cleanin', the air thick wi' the smell o' coal and oil.

The runs tae Inverness and Wick were tough but rewarding. The scenery along the route was spectacular, and despite the lang hours, there was a sense o' accomplishment every time we completed a journey. We worked hard, but we also knew how tae make the best o' it. Those steam engine breakfasts were a highlight, a small moment o' comfort in the midst o' a gruellin' day.

One day, I left Paddington, and it took me sixteen and a half hours tae get tae Plymouth. I had only one engine because the other engine was knackered, and the front engine was fucked. The engine at the back was pushin' me all the way through because I had nae power in the front, and it kept gaun. The engineer came along and said, "Oh, we'll hook ye up wi' an engine." By the time they got me hooked up, I was three miles outside fuckin' Plymouth. I said tae him, "Do nae fuckin' bother, pal. I'm through tae Plymouth. There's nae point in givin' me an engine now. Just change that when I get intae bloody Plymouth."

I had aboot five or six different managers come and go, come and go. A lot o' the drivers didna like a lot o' the area managers. The drivers all got on well; we were a good bunch. There were a few Scottish boys. I worked in the only Scottish depot in the whole o' Kent—Sly Green. There were nae Irish, nae Welsh, nae English, just Scots in that depot then. The area manager, the drivers, the guards, the shunters, and the track lane gang, they were all Scottish lads. When the Scottish depots started closin', ye used tae pick up yer P45 and move tae the next depot. I worked in aboot sixty or seventy depots, if nae more. I started in Kyle o' Lochalsh. The best train ye'll ever get is the Highlander. It goes o'er the viaduct, the one they used for Harry Potter.

ON AND OFF THE RAILS

They got paid like £150,000 a time for that engine tae go.

I wasnae in Harry Potter, but I was on Cracker! Wi' Robbie Coltrane. I was in the very first episode, wi' a' the blood a' ower the coaches. There had tae be a British Rail driver, and I was a class driver. I was sittin' spare at Victoria, so they gied me a taxi up tae Berry tae drive this engine. It wasnae real blood in the coaches, just sprayed-on water paint stuff. There was supposed tae be a murder on the coaches, and I was the driver. I got three minutes that was cut doon tae seven seconds! The driver o' the very first train on Cracker.

Robbie Coltrane comes frae Buckie in Scotland. He came on one day wi' a posh voice, and I said, "Awa' wi' ye, ya fat bastard. I ken ye're a country laddie like me, arenae ye?" He just fuckin' looked at me and said, "Where are ye fae?" I said, "Huntly." He used tae eat a double dinner; he had double plates. He was a right fat greedy bastard. He could make food disappear, God almighty. I did five days on that for my seven seconds. I wouldnae forget that. I got fifty quid a day and got a' my meals paid for me.

The trains were a private company, but they werenae allowed tae drive on British Rail tracks without a British driver, so they had tae get an official driver tae drive the engine. It was alright. I was just sittin' playin' cards wi' one o' the drivers. I wasnae excited tae be there, really. It was just a job tae me. I didnae give a monkeys. Ye were sittin' around a lot. I used tae sit in the cabin in the train, and ye'd get a few punters comin' up tae ye. I'd tell them tae piss off. I never changed my attitude towards anyone. I dinnae give a monkeys, me.

I got in a lot o' fights on the rails, if I'm, honest with ya. picked up an area manager one day in Brighton, and he was gobbin' aff at me. I was like, "Who the hell dae ye think ye're talkin' tae, ya wanker!" I grabbed him and held him up in the air by the throat. He was taken away tae hospital efter that, but he survived. I didnae kill the bastard! I've been assaulted, I've been stabbed on the trains. I was stabbed in the throat at Leeds. They had tae

ON AND OFF THE RAILS

keep ma throat closed in the ambulance. The blood was pissin' oot everywhere. They took me doon tae Jimmy's in Leeds. Jimmy Savile himself wheeled me oot o' the ambulance and intae the theatre.

The bloke that stabbed me moved in doon the road frae me and I didnae realise for a lang time. I took ma dog for a walk one day, and I went doon the road, doon the back o' the hooses, tae brin' the dog for a run around the fields, and this bastard was in his garden. I'm lookin' at him, and I said, "I fuckin' know him." I went back home and was goin' again, and ma missus said, "Where are ye goin' now?" I said, "I'm gaun tae sort oot that bastard who stabbed me."

I had loads o' arguments wi' the managers in the railways. They always threatened tae suspend me, but they never did. This bloke, when I used tae drive frae Brighton up tae London, I came in one mornin' aboot eight, and this bloke was on the platform wi' an umbrella. He kept pokin' me in the face wi' it. I said, "Ye poke me once mair, ya bastard, and I'll fuckin' flatten ya." He poked me again, so I just jammed the brakes, jumped through the fuckin' cabin, and whacked him straight across the jaw. He was oot like a light doon on the fuckin' platform. They were shoutin' my name, "Driver Scatterty, report tae the area manager! Driver Scatterty, report tae the area manager!" I went up tae him and said, "What the fuck is gaun on?" He said, "Did ye hit a passenger?" I said, "Aye." He said, "Why?" I said, "Because he wouldnaestop pokin' me in the face wi' his fuckin' umbrella. He could have fuckin' blinded me." "Ye're not supposed tae hit passengers." "Well, what should I dae? Wait till he fuckin' blinds me, like? Ye fuckin' asshole."

Oh, my area manager never knew what the fuck was gaun on in Victoria. By the time I got oot there and up tae Clapham Junction, all the trains had stopped. Every train frae Brighton tae London, frae the North tae London, everywhere had stopped. Everybody—all the drivers and guards—walked aff and left all the passengers off the train because all the trains had stopped because I had been suspended for whackin' a passenger. They

ON AND OFF THE RAILS

reinstated me within three hours. The manager rang me frae Clapham Junction station and said, "They want ye back in Victoria, Bill. Ye've got a taxi waitin' at the door for ye." So I got a taxi back tae Victoria, and they reinstated me within three hours. "Here," he said, "get back tae fuckin' work. Ye caused me untold problems!" I said, "Why?" He said, "Well, all the fuckin' trains were stopped." I said, "I wonder why they had nae moved frae Clapham Junction!" Cos nothin' moved! I just stood there and laughed, and he said, "Ye think this is funny?" I said, "I think it's fuckin' hilarious." I didnae care, either. I didnae care a monkeys. But I was outspoken then, and I've been outspoken all my life.

The area manager was a wanker, and I didnae get on with him at the best o' times. The rows I used to have with him! I threw him across the desk one day because he got on my bastard nerves. I said, "Are ye glad to see me going? Nae more throwin' ye on the fuckin' desk now, is there?" I got loads o' warnings, red warnings, threats to suspend me and all the rest o' it, but it never came off. I mean, he threatened to send me home one day, and I said, "Ah, fine. I'll do what I fuckin' want to rather than put up with an asshole like you," and I just fuckin' walked out the office. I slammed the door, and the glass panel on the door fuckin' broke. I slammed the door, and fuckin' crash! There was glass lyin' all over the floor, and the area manager went, "Ye broke my door!" I said, "Ah, fuck off, ya pillock!" and just walked out the office. Everybody was standin' there killin' themselves laughin' because they thought it was hilarious. He didnae though. He didnae think it was funny. He was one o' these wankers that came straight from college and university and all that. I dinnae know what he was daein'at the railway. I told him that one day. I said to him in front o' everyone, "If I give ye a fiver, will ye get away from the fuckin' railway?" He said, "How dare ye talk to me like that." I said, "Ah, bugger off!"

The day I retired, I finished at quarter past three and came down through Paddington. I had left Paddington around ten o'clock in the mornin' and

ON AND OFF THE RAILS

didnae even realise it was my last day! When I got into Plymouth, there were loads o' people on the platform, and I was thinking, "Fuckin' hell, there's loads waitin' to get on this bloody train." I jumped out, and another driver jumped out in front o' me and headed off. So I grabbed my bag, had it around my shoulder, and walked out onto the platform. All these people were comin' towards me, with their suits and bowties and all this shite. I'm going, "Fuckin' hell, they must all be goin' to some posh do somewhere."

The area manager came up and shook my hand. I said, "Why? What the fuck is goin' on?" He said, "This is yer last day, isnae it?" I said, "Oh, is it? If ye say so, like." He goes, "Dinnae ye know you're retiring?" I said, "Ah, I know I was retirin' sometime, but I didnae know when." He handed me a glass o' champagne. It tasted like shite, so I fuckin' threw it in the bin. It tasted like piss water. I said, "Piss is fuckin' stronger than that, man." He fuckin' walked off and wouldnae speak to me after that! He was a

WILLIAM SCATTERTY

wanker anyway. All me rail managers, I used to call them all the bastard names under the sun.

Despite the daft managers, I have to admit, I was a wee bit sad to be leaving. I realised that was the end o' my railway career, and it shocked me a bit. I wasnae expectin' it. The reality hit me that I'd never again feel the vibration o' the rails beneath my feet or hear the comfortin' clatter o' the wheels on the tracks. A chapter o' my life was closing, and a big part o' me was reluctant to let it go. But as always, I faced it head-on, no regrets, and ready for whatever came next.

COURTSHIP AND COMMITMENT

I was seventeen when I met ma wife. We went together for a year, then I got married at eighteen. We were together for twenty-eight years, and I canae complain really—it was alright! She really was a bonnie lass. She had this gorgeous smile that could light up a room, and she had a heart as big as her smile.

Ma wife passed away in 2000 fae cancer. That was a tough time. She's buried next tae oor son, just a wee thing o' ashes in the cemetery in Loe Houses. I visit them often, though it never gets any easier. She was a Yorkshire lassie, and she's restin' in Yorkshire. There's a certain peace in knowin' she's back in her homeland, but it doesnae take away the

ON AND OFF THE RAILS

ache o' missin' her. Every time I visit, I brin' a bunch o' her favourite flowers and sit by her grave, talkin' to her as if she could hear me. Maybe she can, who knows?

Life without her has never been the same. Aye, we had oor ups and downs, like any couple, but she was ma rock, ma anchor. Even after all these years, I still find masel' turnin' to tell her somethin' or lookin' for her in a crowd. She might be gone, but she'll always be a part o' me..

When we met, I was a train driver oot o' Huddersfield depot as a trainee driver. We were all in the pub one day, havin' a few jars, and this lass from the office came in to get a drink. So I said to her, "D'ye want a drink?" and she says, "Aye, are ye buying?" I says, "Aye, I'll buy ye a fuckin' drink; I'm no tight bastard." And so I bought the drink and started chattin' to Angie, and we got together that way. We were just friends at first, and then it went from there.

When I saw her for the first time, I thought, "Ah, she's nae bad looking!" She said, "Why are ye lookin' at me?" I said, "Well, ye are better lookin' than the rest o' them, arenae ya? You're out with a bunch o' gnomes." I tell the truth; the others didnae like me very much.

I wasnae nervous about askin' her out. I said, "D'ye fancy goin' for a pint?" She says, "Aye," and I says, "Right ye are." Her friends said, "Dinnae go out with him," they didnae like me very much. I called them yoyos and everything. But I say it like it is! I'm damn straight with everybody.

Angie and I, we had a grand time together. She had a wicked sense o' humour and could keep up with my banter. We went from sharin' pints to sharin' our lives. Aye, it was a whirlwind romance, but it felt right. She had a laugh that could lift yer spirits, even on the shittiest days. We'd sit and talk for hours about everythin' and nothing. It was easy, bein' with her. She made life lighter, somehow.

Our first date, we went tae the pictures. We were snoggin' in the back seats, so I cannae remember what movie was on. The woman came along wi' her torch and said, "Go way and get out, ye dirty bastards!" She said, "Get out, get out, get out!" They threw us oot. I demanded my fuckin' money back; I only saw half the film. Not even that really.

One time we went tae see a creepy film, wi' ghosts and that, and we were all shoutin' at the screen, "Look out behind you, look out!" and we all got kicked oot at three in the mornin'. We used tae get up tae all sorts o' mischief.

Angie had a great sense o' humour, and we'd be laughin' about it all the way back hame. We'd go to the chippy for a late-night snack, sittin' on a bench, eatin' chips and talkin' about everythin' under the stars.

When Angie took me down tae meet her mother for the first time, it was quite the event. Her mother looked me up and doon, then says, "Oh, ye seem tae be a nice lad. Whereabouts in Yorkshire do ye come from?" I said, "I dinnae come from Yorkshire; I come from Scotland." Fuckin' hell! All hell broke loose.

WILLIAM SCATTERTY

She really didnae like me from that day onwards. "You're not marryin' my daughter," she says, "you're not good enough!" I says, "Ah, go way and fuck out o' that, ya silly old bastard." We used to shout and scream at one another. Every time we met, it was like World War Three.

Her dad, on the other hand, was great—a nicer bloke ye couldnae have met. He was a joiner. We used tae go for a pint and everythin' together. But her mother? She was just an auld bastard. We never got on—just war every time we saw each other.

Her mother wouldnae let me in the house; I had to kick the door in a few times. Her father secretly gave me a key, but she changed the locks every time. I ended up wi' ten different keys tae get into the fuckin' house. She was a right miserable cow. She's dead now, fuckin' long gone. The poor bastards up there have tae put up wi' her now.

It was always World War Three when we used tae get together. A Sunday afternoon dinner, and we'd never even eat the meal. The food would sit on the table while we yelled and cursed at each other. Angie and her dad would sit there, caught in the middle o' the battlefield, tryin' tae keep the peace. Angie would give me a look that said, "Please, just this once, try not to provoke her." But it was impossible; the woman had it in for me.

Despite all the chaos, Angie and I stayed strong. We loved each other, and nothin' her mother did could change that. We'd leave her parents' house, hand in hand, laughin' about the latest skirmish. Angie would say, "Ye handled that well," and I'd reply, "Aye, well, it takes a tough Scot to deal wi' an angry Yorkshirewoman." We built our life together, despite her mother's constant interference. Our love was stronger than any feud, and we made it work.

Angie had been workin' for a firm in Huddersfield, daein'office work. Her boss was a miserable old bastard. One day, I went in an' said, "If ye ever speak tae Angie like that again, I'll put ye in intensive care, ye cunt." He threatened tae sack her. I said, "If ye sack her, I'll punch yer lights out," so he didn't. She enjoyed me standin' up for her. I went in tae see her in the office, and they wouldnae let me past. I pulled the boss over the counter, smacked his head off the counter a couple o' times, and said, "Go get her." But he just fell down on the floor, unconscious. So I walked over the counter and went in tae see her. When I came back out, he was still out cold. They had tae use smellin' salts tae brin' him round. I got banned from the office after that!

She used tae go oot on a Saturday night wi' her girlfriends, and I would go oot wi' the boys. We'd get boozy and then meet up in the middle o' toon and come hame together. I was in love wi' her, simple as that. We used tae see each other a couple o' times a week, and at the weekend. She'd come tae me on a Friday night and stay wi' me until Sunday. Her mother used tae come round on a Saturday tryin' tae get her tae go back hame. So I threw her oot o' the hoose a couple o' times. I had tae chuck her oot.

I was livin' in a flat in Huddersfield then. It was a wee place but cosy enough. Then I moved frae there tae Milltown, which was a brilliant place. It had a great sense o' community, and the folk were friendly. When we got married, she moved in wi' me.

I was so dedicated tae Angie. We did everythin' together, and her mum didnae like it one bit. At our wedding, when the minister stood up and said, "Any person here who thinks these two shouldnae get married," I looked straight at her mum and said, "If ye open yer fuckin' mouth, I'll put ma boot in it!" So she kept her mouth shut. Ah, I'm o' a gentle persuasion, ye ken.

That day we got married was a big fuckin' riot, with the actual riot squad and everythin' there. I'm the only guy who got married with a riot squad at my weddin' and four policemen. We all started fighting, and the Yorkshire folks didnae like Scotsmen, so I just waded in and said, "Ye take that, oh yes!" Oh, it was a good wedding! I was only eighteen, but I got stuck in with the rest o' them. I got arrested, locked up for the night, then they let me out about two in the morning. The bobby asked

WILLIAM SCATTERTY

me, "Are ye the bridegroom?" I said, "Oh, aye, I am." He said, "Well, ye ought to show an example." I replied, "Oh fuckin' hell, ye havenae got all them bastards locked up! I'm showin' them an example." I was fightin' with three bobbies, four bystanders, the barman, the manager, and the bloke that was puttin' the marquee up. The marquee man did nothing; he was just there. I asked him to move and he wouldn't, so I punched him. A good day was had by all! Oh, I'm a nice man now though—a very, very nice man.

I had ma kilt on, a full Scottish rig-out, and she had a beautiful bridal dress. She was gorgeous. I've no photos left, but I remember it all in my head. I've moved around so much I've lost a lot o' photos. Angie didnae work at all after we got married. I told her she could carry on workin' if she liked; it was up to her. But I had enough money to pay for the two o' us, so it ended up that was what she wanted to do.

We settled into married life, makin' the best o' what we had. Our wee flat was cosy, and Angie

ON AND OFF THE RAILS

made it feel like a proper home. She had a knack for makin' everythin' look nice, addin' wee touches here and there that made all the difference. We enjoyed our time together, sharin' laughs and makin' memories. She was my rock, and I was hers. Those were the best years, despite the chaos and the fights. We were happy, and that's what mattered.

My wife's dad was a joiner, so he was oot most o' the day, leavin' me tae deal wi' the dreaded mother-in-law who used tae come over tae my hoose all the time. Every time I came hame frae work and saw her there, I'd get a right scunner. She came roond tae keep Angie company, but I couldna stand it. One time, she bought me a tie. If ye've never seen an ugly tie, this one took the cake. It was the ugliest tie ye could imagine. God almighty! I chucked it straight in the fuckin' bin. She asked, "Where's yer tie?" I said, "It's in the fuckin' bin. If ye want it, ye can have it!"

We moved around the country a fair bit, leavin' Huddersfield. I was transferred tae the depot there, but they moved me around often. I kept ma hoose in Huddersfield, but we just sort o' dossed about gettin' flats here and there. British Rail had flats and housin' and everythin' for their staff anyway, so we used tae go in one o' them. The flats and houses were all furnished. We got coal from the depot; we used tae get bags for the coal fire. The houses were nice and warm.

We had tae move often, ten or twenty odd times. When a depot closed, ye got the option o' pickin' yer P45 up or movin' tae the next depot, so I just moved from depot tae depot. Angie was a bit pissed off wi' all the movin' after about ten, fifteen years. She said, "Nah, I'm goin' back to Huddersfield."

"Aye, but what about me?" I asked her.

"Ye can stay in the flats if ye like, but I'm fed up wi' it," she replied.

Angie made it clear that she wanted some stability, and I couldna blame her. It wasnae easy, all that moving. I mean, I was travellin' tae London all the time. I'd finish ma night shift in London by six

ON AND OFF THE RAILS

or seven in the mornin' and catch the first train north, get off at Wakefield, then take a local train intae Huddersfield, and finally get a bus hame from Huddersfield station. The buses I used tae take were the 207. I'd jump on that; the driver never took a fare or anything. He'd say, "Aye, mate, on ye go," because I was always in ma uniform gettin' on the bus anyway. The drivers and conductors never took ma fare. Same wi' London Transport; when ye travel around London, ye never paid yer fare. I put ma hand out one day and said, "Here mate, do ye want ma fare?" and he says, "Nah, you're alright."

I used tae travel tae Huddersfield from Leeds, and sometimes I'd need tae get out at Leeds city centre and get a bus up tae Neville Hill tae pick up a train. I'd jump on and say, "Neville Hill, mate," and he'd say, "Aye, okay," and he used tae give me the money back. That was Yorkshire Rider drivers. Same when I was in Glasgow. I used tae live in East Kilbride in the multi-storeys there. I'd get a bus, the 68, tae the south side o' Glasgow. It would go from East Kilbride and terminate at the bus station. It used tae come by ma estate. The driver would come wake me up about two or three in the mornin' and say, "Yer stop, mate," and I'd say, "Cheers for wakin' me up." They all used tae look at me like I was drunk or something—the whole bus full o' people.

The drivers were alright for that. I'd get a coffee in the mornin' goin' hame, and sometimes I'd get ma breakfast on the buffet car. Occasionally, I'd get a taxi hame, and the same driver would pick me up at Wakefield. One day, I finally looked at him closely and said, "I fuckin' know you." He said, "Aye, I'm yer neighbour, ye fuckin' cunt. I'll drop ye off and park up for the night then." He drove me hame and then was like, "I'm signin' off now, bye!" and that was it.

Oh, aye, yeah. I didnae spend much time at hame; I was mostly out on the road. I missed the time at hame, but that was the life o' a railwayman. Constantly on the move, always headin' somewhere, and never stayin' put for long. It was a life filled with endless journeys, early mornings, and late nights.

ON AND OFF THE RAILS

Me and the missus didnae get tae spend a lot o' quality time together, truth be told. We spent our honeymoon in Somerset. We went doon tae Devon because I liked the steam train. She wouldnae come wi' me on the steam train at first, so I said, "I'm gaun on ma own then." So she said, "Alright, I'll come wi' ya." We went tae Devon tae see the railways—the first steam train I went on. We didnae go on many holidays abroad; we mostly stayed in the UK. We bought a caravan in Boness, and the engine blew up. It went bang in the middle o' Yodel. The missus said, "There's smoke comin' oot the bonnet, oot the front o' the van." I said, "Nah, ye must be seein' things." All o' a sudden, there was a loud bang, and a fuckin' blimp flew oot the top o' the caravan head, and the engine just fell through the bottom onto the road. We were stuck like that until a mechanic came along and towed me tae the garage. I said, "Can ye put the engine back?" He said, "No, it's beyond repair, mate." I said, "What can ye do?" He said, "There's a scrapyard doon there!" I said, "Alright," and I got a fiver for scrap!

WILLIAM SCATTERTY

One time we did go tae Spain on holiday. We went tae Tenerife, Benidorm, and Alicante. I was about nineteen then; it was back in the eighties. We just fancied Spain for a holiday, but I lost my rag wi' the missus in Spain, in Tenerife, because this bloke was there, and he was daein'this trick where ye put somethin' under a cardboard cup and move it around. I was watchin' him, and the missus won a few bob. Then she started losing. I was watchin' this cunt, so I pulled him up by the throat and said, "You're a swindlin' bastard, you," but he couldnae speak English. I pinned him against the wall, and the gendarme, the Spanish police, came up and arrested me for assault. I said, "You're a cheap bastard; he's a tourist attraction. He's a cheat!" But they couldnaeunderstand me. I said, "Do ye know what keeps yer ears apart?" He said, "No." I said, "Yer bollocks," and he understood that! My wife said tae me, "Ye affronted me today."

That holiday was a right mess, but we had some laughs. Spain was hot as hell, and the food was grand, but I always missed the cool air and proper

ON AND OFF THE RAILS

grub back home. The missus enjoyed it more than I did, I think. She liked the sunbathin' and the wee shops. I just wanted tae get a pint and watch the world go by. Spain was alright, but it never really felt like home. We didnae go back again after that. We stuck tae the UK, where I could understand the buggers and they could understand me.

Durin' our time at home, we mostly used to go oot on the weekends. We'd head oot places, go visitin' and that. The missus had a lot o' friends. We'd often go for a pint together, and while they sat in the house drinkin' tea and coffee, we'd head tae the pub and have a few bevvies. A lot o' her friends had drivers for husbands; it was all railway staff I used tae meet up wi'. Very, very few other people I used tae meet up wi'—it was all railway lads.

The weekends were grand. We'd start at the local pub, usually the one down the road, and we'd have a few laughs. The railway lads were a good bunch, always up for a bit o' banter. We'd swap stories about the week's work, the close calls on the tracks, and the daft things passengers would get up tae. Angie would join in sometimes, but she preferred tae chat with the other wives and have a laugh about us blokes.

We'd often end the night at someone's house, carryin' on wi' the drinks and havin' a good time. Angie and her friends would sit in the kitchen, natterin' away, while us lads stayed in the livin' room, pints in hand, talkin' shite until the early hours. It was a simple life, but it was good. We were a tight-knit community, and the railway was more than just a job; it was a way o' life.

Angie liked tae visit her friends' houses, especially when their husbands were on the same shifts as me. They'd gossip and catch up on all the latest news, while we'd enjoy the rare break from the hard graft. I never minded the visiting; it gave me a chance tae unwind and enjoy some company after a long week on the rails.

Even when the weeks were tough, and the job seemed like it would never end, I always had the weekends wi' Angie tae look forward to. We made the best o' what we had, and in those simple pleasures, we found our happiness.

We got married young, but we made it work. Angie was my partner in crime, my confidante, my best friend. Even after a long, hard day on the rails, comin' home to her made it all worth it. We built a life together, had our ups and downs, but we always had each other's backs. I miss her every day, but I carry her with me, in every laugh, every memory, every moment. She's still with me, in a way. Angie was a light in my life, always makin' the dark times seem brighter. We shared so many laughs and made so many memories. Even now, I can hear her laughter, see her smile, and it brings a warmth to my heart. She was my world, and I was hers.

THE WEIGHT O' LOVE AND LOSS

My son Adam was born in 1978 and died in 1987. He was just nine years old when he was shot—shot through the head. The bloke who lived next door tae me was a gun fanatic. He used tae keep an air rifle. I grew up on a fairm and knew how tae handle a gun. Everybody knows ye dinnae carry a loaded gun over yer shoulder. This cunt had the gun loaded, and it went off, straight through my son's head. He lived for eighteen hours after but died in Jimmy's in Leeds.

I remember the day like it was yesterday. We were in the garden, Adam playin' about, full o' life and mischief. That daft bastard next door was always tinkerin' with his air rifles, actin' like he was

ON AND OFF THE RAILS

some sort o' sharpshooter. We all heard the bang. It echoed through the street, sendin' a chill right doon ma spine. I ran over, and there was Adam. I screamed for help, for somebody tae call an ambulance, but in my heart, I knew it was bad— really bad.

They rushed Adam tae the hospital, and those eighteen hours felt like an eternity. I sat by his side, holdin' his wee hand, prayin' for a miracle. The doctors did their best, but there was nothin' they could do. The bullet had done too much damage. When they told me he was gone, it was like my world had ended. My beautiful boy, gone because o' a stupid, careless mistake.

The bastard next door claimed it was an accident, said he didnae mean tae do it. But an accident or not, it didnae brin' Adam back. The court gave him nine months probation and banned him from ever holdin' a firearm again. That was it. Nine months for takin' my son's life. When he came out o' court, I was waitin' for him. I whacked the bastard with one o' those big T-bars, broke both his arms and legs. He fell down in a heap outside the court door. There were two bobbies standin' there. I thought they might arrest me, but they said, "We didnae see nothing, mate," and told me to fuck off now that I'd had my revenge.

I never saw that bastard again. He moved away, and good riddance. If I ever did see him, I'd probably kill him. The rage and sorrow have never left me. The pain never really goes away. It's always there, gnawin' at the edges o' my heart.

Losin' Adam was the hardest thing I've ever had tae endure. It changed me, made me angrier, more bitter. But I had tae keep going, for Angie and for maself. The memory o' Adam, his laughter, his cheeky smile, that's what keeps me going. He may be gone, but he'll never be forgotten. Every day, I carry his memory with me.

When my wife told me she was pregnant, I was over the moon tae be a dad. I told her tae stop drinkin' and smoking, and she did, bless her. The day he was born the manager said tae me, "Ye better go home; I think yer wife is ready to drop." I

ON AND OFF THE RAILS

jumped off the train, and they had a new driver ready at London Bridge for me. I got a train from London Bridge, a taxi to Wakefield, and my neighbour, a taxi driver, picked me up from Wakefield and drove me to Huddersfield General. The railway paid for most o' it. By the time I got there, Adam was born.

The dreaded mother-in-law was there too. She said, "I'm here to see my grandchild." I said, "Okay, you've seen him; now fuck off." She said, "You're not a very nice man." I said, "No, I am a very, very nice man. Now fuck off." We just never found a way to get on.

We brought Adam home in the taxi, a wee bundle o' joy wrapped up in blankets. Life changed a bit after that. I quietened down. Angie didnae like me bein' away because I'd be gone for a week at a time. I would stay with my mum and sister in Surrey if I was far away, drivin' in London, Redhill, Drumbridge, and places like that. I was there all week and then home at the weekends.

142

WILLIAM SCATTERTY

Comin' home tae Angie and Adam became the highlight o' my week. Adam was a lively wee bairn, always laughin' and kickin' aboot. I remember his first steps, the way he'd toddle around the house, fallin' and gettin' back up again with a big grin on his face. I'd scoop him up and swin' him around, his giggles fillin' the room. Angie would watch us, smiling, happy in those moments.

Those weekends were precious, filled with family time and laughter. We'd go to the park, have picnics, and I'd push Adam on the swings, his little legs pumpin' with excitement. At night, I'd read him stories until he fell asleep in my arms. Life felt perfect in those moments, the three o' us together, makin' memories.

But it was hard bein' away from them durin' the week. I missed seein' Adam grow, missed Angie's companionship. I'd call home every night, just to hear their voices, to feel connected even when I was miles away. Angie was a rock, managin' everythin' while I was gone. She never complained,

ON AND OFF THE RAILS

just got on with it, lookin' after Adam and keepin' the house runnin' smoothly.

When Adam got a bit older, he'd wait up for me to come home on Fridays. As soon as he heard the door, he'd come running, throwin' himself into my arms. Those hugs were the best part o' my week, the love and joy in his eyes makin' all the hard days worth it.

Adam was a lovely little gardener. He had such a passion for growin' flowers. He'd go into the supermarkets with his mother, wander off, and look at the packets o' seeds. He'd come back with packets and give them to his mum. She'd say, "Oh, ye found more seeds," and he'd say, "Yes, can I plant them?" She'd always say, "Aye, ye can."

He used to be in the garden for hours, diggin' holes and plantin' the seeds with such care. The flowers came up beautifully! He had a knack for it, a green thumb that seemed almost magical. He knew what plantin' was, better than I did, and I was born and brought up on a fairm! He knew every name o' every flower he planted, rattlin' them off like a wee botanist. He was very clever, our Adam.

I remember him in his little wellies, dirt smudged on his cheeks, a look o' pure concentration as he tended to his garden. He'd chat away to the flowers, tellin' them to grow strong and tall. And they did. His flowers were always the best in the neighbourhood, a burst o' colour and life that brightened up our days.

It's hard tae think about, him bein' so young, only nine when he died. It's a pain that never really goes away. Every time I see a flower, I think o' him, o' his little hands plantin' the seeds, o' his excitement when the first sprouts appeared. He had so much life in him, so much love for the simple things. His garden was his pride and joy, and it brought so much joy to us as well.

Those years were some o' the happiest o' my life. Despite the distance and the time apart, we were a family, strong and full o' love. Adam brought so much light into our lives, and Angie and I cherished every moment we had with him.

ON AND OFF THE RAILS

When Adam died, my missus got written up in Yorkshire TV, the Sun, the Star, and the Mirror. She got compensation from all o' them. The shite they printed was unbelievable. That guy on Yorkshire TV was an ugly bastard. On TV, he was always smart, right? But ye should've seen him comin' in the morning—scruffy as hell. All done up nicely for the TV camera. I said, "You're an ugly fat bastard, arenae ye?" He said, "Ye canae say that!" I said, "I can! Look at the state o' ye. I'm only tellin' the truth."

The stories they printed were a load o' shite. They claimed we were never there for our son, which was bollocks. We had a neighbour, Denis, who was about four foot ten. The Sun guy went to see him, wantin' the story off him. The guy started pokin' the camera in his face, and Denis said, "If ye dinnae fuck off from my door, I'll be throwin' this camera," and true to his word, he threw the camera over the fence, and it landed in the road. He said, "If ye dinnae fuck off from my door, you'll be followin' it." Old Denis was a weightlifter, and he picked the bloke up and hurled him. He cleared the garden fence, the road, and landed in the green outside my door. He had a broken leg, a broken arm, a broken nose, and five teeth missing. Aye, he was taken away to the hospital in an ambulance.

We had so many reporters harassin' us. They never left us alone. The police moved us out o' the house for a few weeks and told all the reporters to get away. I thumped quite a few o' those bastards. I hammered one or two o' them. I got two o' them together in a headlock and banged their heads together. They slid down to the floor. The bobby said, "What happened there?" I said, "I think they fell over, mate." The bobby said, "Yeah right, I didnae see it, mate." Yorkshire police are alright. They're decent.

It was a sad day when I had to go and identify Adam's body. I went mad with the undertaker. When he took the body out to go in the back o' the hearse, I said, "For fuck's sake, he can go in the back seat; he's only nine years old for Christ's sake!" The undertaker just looked at me, and I grabbed him by

ON AND OFF THE RAILS

the fuckin' throat. I had him against the side o' the van. I said, "Ye dinnae fuckin' do what you're told." He was shakin' like a leaf, and the driver was saying, "I dinnae blame you, man." Adam was cremated.

The loss o' Adam hit us hard. He was just nine, for Christ's sake. Seein' him like that, havin' to identify his body, and then dealin' with all the bullshit from the media—it was too much. But we got through it, somehow. Losin' Adam was that. We lost a baby girl before him, around three or four months along. It would have been a boy and a girl. We did try for another kid, but we never got pregnant again.

Things went from bad to worse when Angie started takin' stomach pains in 1999. She wouldnae go to the doctors—she was a bit like me, couldnae be bothered with doctors. I dragged her in the end and said, "Can ye examine her? She's complainin' o' stomach pains." They ran tests and couldnaefind anythin' wrong. They underwent other tests in the hospital, and that's when they found out she had pancreatic cancer. They gave her six months. She was young when she died—forty-six years old. We were both eighteen when we got married and were together for twenty-eight years.

Watchin' Angie suffer was heart-wrenching. She tried to stay strong, but the pain was relentless. I remember sittin' by her bedside, holdin' her hand, and feelin' utterly helpless. The doctors did what they could, but we both knew it was a losin' battle. Every day, she got weaker, and all I could do was be there for her.

We talked a lot durin' those last months. She'd reminisce about the good times, our honeymoon in Somerset, the steam trains in Devon, and the caravan in Boness. Despite everything, she managed to smile, saying, "Remember the time the engine blew up? We were stuck in the middle o' nowhere, and ye thought I was seein' things when I saw the smoke!" We'd laugh, even in the face o' such a cruel disease.

Her mother, the dreaded mother-in-law, came around more often, tryin' to make amends in her own way. There were still tensions, but Angie

ON AND OFF THE RAILS

wanted peace. I tried my best to keep things civil, for her sake. Angie was always the peacemaker, even when she was at her weakest.

The day she passed was the hardest o' my life. I held her hand until her last breath, whisperin' that I loved her and that everythin' would be alright. When she finally let go, I felt like a part o' me had died with her. She was my rock, my best friend, and suddenly, she was gone.

Even the day o' the funeral, we had a fuckin' punch-up because her mother kept interfering. At the crematorium, some o' her family turned up. They never came to see her while she was alive. I said, "Where have ye been the last ten years? Do ye think by comin' here you're goin' to get money off her? Ye can fuck off." I was grabbin' them by the throat and throwin' them out o' the crematorium. The minister came after them and asked, "What's goin' on?" I said, "I dinnae want them here. Can ye remove the front row there? Can ye remove the fuckin' lot o' them? I dinnae want them in here." He said, "I canae really do that." I said, "Well, ye do that, or I'll get the police in to remove them." So, he asked them politely to go, and they all stood outside the door o' the crematorium.

I went down to watch Angie be cremated and ended up smackin' every one o' them, tellin' them to fuck off. The police turned up and asked what was goin' on. I said, "You'll have to ask them. They werenae invited, and I've asked them to leave." They were pickin' themselves off the deck. One fell over, and the bobby started laughing, saying, "She's got a black eye, and his nose is bent." I said, "Well, he must have climbed over the fence and fell over." He looked at me and walked away. He said, "Just ask them to go, get in the car, and leave." The police sat there until they all left. Then we went back to the house for the wake. I got absolutely fuckin' drunk as a cunt!

Her mother was there. I threatened to throw her out the window, and that window was not open, mind you! Someone said, "Ye canae do that, Bill, you're drunk, man." I said, "I dinnae give a fuck." Her dad just walked away; he didnae want to know.

ON AND OFF THE RAILS

He was affronted by his wife's behaviour. It was just one o' those things. I told her not to come back to the house again. My missus is gone, so ye stay away. I dinnae want ye back here. She came back twice. I slammed the door in her face. The second time, she stood too close to the door, and when I slammed it, there was blood on the step. She never came back after that. I never saw her again, but she is dead and gone now. Her dad is dead and gone too. I go and see her dad's grave. He's buried just up the road in Peter on Firth.

The wake was a right mess. I was tryin' to drown my sorrows, but I just ended up gettin' more angry. Her mother caused so much stress, even in death. I sat with my mates, drinkin' and reminiscin' about the good times. Angie deserved better than this chaos. I looked around at the people who truly cared, who had been there for us, and I felt a mix o' sorrow and gratitude. I knew I had to carry on, for her memory and for maself, but it was a struggle. Losin' Angie was like losin' a part o' my soul. The house felt emptier, the days longer, and the nights colder. But I had to keep going. That's what she would have wanted.

My son and his mum are buried together. They're buried in the cemetery at Fanny Lane, Lowerhouses Kirkyard. It's just a wee kirkyard in the middle o' the countryside. My son would be forty-seven this year. My wife would be the same age as me—seventy-two. I suppose in a way, I am glad they're together. They're buried together—mum and son.

Losin' them both has left a gapin' hole in my heart, but their gravesite is a place o' solace, a place where I can remember the love we shared. It's a reminder o' the family we once were and the love that still binds us, even in death.

LIFE OFF THE RAILS

After the deaths o' my son and wife, I got the fuck out o' Huddersfield. I upped sticks and left about a week after the funeral. I just took all the stuff I wanted and told the in-laws I didnae care what happened to the house. They could do what they wanted. I said, "I'm off, bye," and went down and stayed with my mum. My father-in-law came to see me a few times. When he died, I went to his funeral and kept my distance from his wife. He was a really good bloke, a decent bloke. He didnae deserve somebody like that. He deserved someone better. She's dead and gone now too.

I stayed with my mum for a while, but after a bit, she was pissed off at me always bein' underfoot. I

ON AND OFF THE RAILS

got a flat o' my own, so I lived on my own. I never really bothered with anybody else after Angie. Since she died, I've been on my own for 24 years. I've never had any inklin' to even have a girlfriend. I just lived life. I dinnae know how long I've got left now.

Livin' alone was a new chapter in my life. It was a mix o' peace and loneliness. I missed Angie and Adam terribly, but I couldnaestay in that house full o' memories. Every corner, every room reminded me o' what I had lost. Movin' in with my mum was a temporary fix, a place to catch my breath, but I knew I needed to stand on my own two feet again.

My flat became my sanctuary. It wasnae much, but it was mine. I filled it with things that mattered to me, memories o' the past and small comforts for the present. I learned to enjoy my own company, findin' solace in the quiet moments. I spent a lot o' time reflecting, thinkin' about the life I had with Angie and Adam, and the life I had now.

I dinnae know how long I've got left now, but I'm alright with that. I've lived a full life, with all its ups and downs. I've had love, loss, and everythin' in

WILLIAM SCATTERTY

between. And in the end, I've made my peace with it all.

I didnae go out very much, but things started to unravel for me around that time. I used to go out with the drivers and have a few bevvies. I used to drink Newcastle Brown Ale. I would think nothin' o' downin' twenty odd fuckin' bottles a day. I was always drunk when I was driving. I used to fall out o' the train car onto the platform. I was that drunk I couldnae stand. I was usin' it to cope with the pain o' the losses. I would drink ale and a half bottle o' whisky every day. I was an alcoholic. I'd go into work drunk and leave drunk. I'd try and get in five, six minutes early so I could go down to the railway club, get a couple o' bottles, hop back on the train, and on to the next station. Ye got 15-20 railway clubs between Victoria and Brighton. I used to drink about twenty bottles goin' down and twenty comin' back. I used to fall out o' the engine. Boomph! Face down on the platform. The drivers would have to pick me up and drag me into the drivers' room. I used to say to the manager, "I was just a bit under the weather," and he'd say, "He's fuckin' drunk!!" "Oh no, just a bit under the weather," but I couldnae maselfstand up, let alone anythin' else.

It wasnae long before ma life started spiralin' oot o' control. Drink became ma way tae numb the pain, tae cope wi' the emptiness left by Angie and Adam. I'd start ma day wi' a couple o' bottles o' Newcastle Brown Ale, and by the end o' the day, I'd have gone through a half bottle o' whisky as well. Ma mates knew the state I was in, but we were all in it together, drownin' our sorrows in the bottom o' a pint glass.

Drivin' the trains, I'd stagger on, barely able tae see straight. Ma uniform was a mess, covered in ale stains, and I'd slur ma words so badly, passengers must've thought I was a right mess. The railway clubs were ma second home, places where I could just disappear into the background, blend in wi' other lads who were just as lost as me. The smell o' stale beer, the clink o' glasses, and the constant hum o' chatter were ma companions.

WILLIAM SCATTERTY

I remember one time, I was so blotto that I stumbled oot o' the engine at Victoria and landed flat on ma face on the platform. The other drivers had tae haul me up and drag me intae the drivers' room. I'd laugh it off, pretendin' it was just a wee mishap, but inside, I was fallin' apart. The manager would shake his head and say, "He's fuckin' drunk!" but I'd just grin and say, "Just a bit under the weather."

It was a vicious cycle. The more I drank, the more I needed to drink to feel anythin' at all. I was lost in a fog o' alcohol, and there were days when I didnae even ken how I managed to drive the train from one end o' the line to the other.

Lookin' back, it's a miracle I didnae cause a serious accident. The drink was a way to escape, but it nearly cost me everything. I was livin' on the edge, one bottle at a time, and it was only a matter o' time before somethin' had to give.

I got in trouble every day wi' work. The other blokes liked the drink as well. Most drivers then were alcoholics. The local pub right beside the

ON AND OFF THE RAILS

depot was run by a lad from Drumchapel. The front door was never open; it was always locked. Ye'd go in the back door. Ye'd come in at two or three in the mornin', and it was fuckin' mobbed. If ye wanted a driver or a guard that wasnae at work, that's where ye found them! I've lost track o' them all. I keep in touch wi' one or two, but most o' the lads I knew are all gone.

The pub was a place where we could let loose and forget about the pressures o' the job. The air was thick wi' the smell o' tobacco and stale beer, the sound o' raucous laughter and clinkin' glasses fillin' the room. It was a tight-knit community, everyone knowin' everyone's business. If ye had a problem, ye'd find a sympathetic ear there, and if ye had somethin' to celebrate, ye'd buy a round for the whole place.

I'd stagger in after a long shift, ma clothes reekin' o' diesel and sweat. The regulars would nod and raise their glasses in greeting, and the barman would already be pourin' ma usual. We'd huddle in groups, sharin' stories and gripes, the camaraderie makin' the grind bearable. We were a band o' brothers, bound by our love for the rails and our need for the bottle.

Aye, I had ma fair share o' run-ins wi' the management. They'd pull me in for meetings, threatenin' suspension, but it never came to that. They needed us more than they cared to admit. We kept the trains running, kept the passengers moving, and despite our flaws, we were damn good at our jobs.

But it wasnae all laughs and pints. The drinkin' took its toll. I watched friends spiral into ruin, their lives fallin' apart as the drink consumed them. Marriages ended, health declined, and some never made it out the other side. I lost track o' many, their faces fadin' into memory. There are times when I wonder what happened to them, but I've learned not to dwell too much on the past. It's too painful.

I used to get pissed, but apart from that, once I stopped drinking, I stopped goin' to the pub. I didnae bother. The doctor said to me one day, "If ye dinnae stop drinking, ye'll be dead in six months,"

ON AND OFF THE RAILS

and I havenae touched a drop for eight years now. I've got a bottle o' whisky in ma fridge; it's been there for two and a half years, and it's still there. I havenae touched it. I can pick the bottle up, put ma hands around it, and it's freezin' from bein' in ma fridge so long. I can touch it, but I wouldnae drink it. I bought it to see if I could tempt maself to drink it, and I have never touched it since.

Quittin' the drink was nae easy. Those first few months were hell. The cravings, the shakes, the nightmares—aye, it was a rough ride. I'd sit in ma flat, starin' at that bottle, darin' maself to take a sip, but I never did. I'd remind maself o' the doctor's words, the faces o' ma lost friends, and the pain o' losin' Angie and Adam. They were the anchors that kept me from driftin' back into that dark sea.

I started to find other ways to fill ma time. I took up gardening, inspired by Adam's love for growin' flowers. I'd spend hours in the garden, tendin' to the plants, watchin' them grow. It brought me a sense o' peace, a connection to ma son. I'd think o' him every time a new flower bloomed, imaginin' the smile on his face.

The railway lads would sometimes drop by, checkin' in on me. They'd brin' stories from the depot, updates on who was daein' what, and the latest gossip. They'd try to get me back out to the pub, but I always declined. I'd offer them a cup o' tea instead, and we'd sit and chat, reminiscin' about the old days.

Life without the drink was a new chapter, a chance to rebuild maself. It wasnae easy, and there were days when I felt like givin' up, but I pushed through. I found strength in the memories o' those I'd lost, in the love I still carried for them. It kept me going, one day at a time.

Now, as I sit here, holdin' that bottle o' whisky, I feel a sense o' pride. I've come a long way from the days o' stumblin' off trains and pickin' fights in pubs. I've learned to find joy in the simple things, to appreciate the quiet moments. And though the scars remain, I've found a way to live with them, to move forward with a clearer mind and a lighter heart.

SEEKIN' ANSWERS

With ma wife and child dead and gone, and havin' given up the drink, I found masel' wi' a lot o' time and silence. The quiet was deafening, and in that silence, the memories o' ma childhood came back tae haunt me. Every night, as I lay in bed, the ghosts o' the past would whisper in ma ear, remindin' me o' the pain and the unanswered questions. The drink had been a way tae drown oot those voices, but now, sober and alone, there was nae escapin' them. The need for answers became a burnin' ache inside me, a need tae understand why I had tae suffer so much, and tae make sure those who wronged me were held accountable.

ON AND OFF THE RAILS

The nights were the worst. I'd lie there, starin' at the ceiling, feelin' the weight o' the darkness pressin' doon on me. Memories I'd tried tae bury for years came floodin' back. The faces o' the bastards who beat me, the cruel laughter o' those who were meant tae care for us weans. It was like they were standin' at the foot o' ma bed, tauntin' me, darin' me tae seek justice. The nightmares were relentless, draggin' me back tae those hellish days in the care home. I could feel the stin' o' the belt, hear the screams o' the other lads, and smell the damp, musty air o' that place.

Sober, the world seemed sharper, the edges more jagged. Every noise, every creak o' the floorboards, would jolt me awake, heart pounding, half expectin' tae see one o' those ghosts from ma past standin' in the doorway. It was in those moments o' terror that I knew I couldnae rest until I got the answers I needed. I had tae ken why I was taken from ma mum, why the social workers and doctors failed me, and why those who inflicted so much pain on us weans were never held accountable.

I started digging, lookin' for records, demandin' answers frae the council and the social work department. They didnae want tae talk, o' course. They threatened me wi' harassment charges, told me tae leave it alone, but I couldnae. I was like a dog wi' a bone, and I was nae lettin' go. I went tae the council offices, shouted ma demands at them, watched as their faces turned pale. They didnae ken what tae do wi' me. I was a man possessed, driven by the need for justice, for closure.

The police tried tae scare me off, but they didnae ken me very well. I told them I'd harass the bastards as much as I wanted, that I'd keep pushin' until I got the truth. The bobbies, some o' them, understood. They saw the fire in ma eyes, the determination. They told me they couldnae blame me, that they'd feel the same in ma shoes. But nae matter how many times they told me tae back off, I kept going.

The truth was all I had left. I needed tae make sure those who wronged me and countless other

ON AND OFF THE RAILS

bairns were held accountable. I wanted tae see them face justice, tae know they couldnae escape what they did. I told the social workers, the doctors, the council – anyone who'd listen – that I'd haunt them when I was gone. I'd drag them intae the fires o' hell if I had tae. They'd never be free o' me, never forget what they did.

In the quiet, in the stillness o' ma sober nights, I found ma purpose. I found the strength tae keep fighting, tae keep demandin' the answers I deserved. And I swore tae masel', nae matter how long it took, I'd get the truth. I'd find peace for masel' and justice for all the bairns who suffered.

I started really workin' hard lookin' for answers about four years ago. I never stopped askin' why the doctors and social workers didnae know I had a paralysed bowel. It was a question that burned in my mind, eatin' away at me. How could they nae see it? It wasnae just ignorance; it was neglect. I needed to ken why they overlooked somethin' so obvious, somethin' that caused me so much pain and misery.

WILLIAM SCATTERTY

The school doctor, she was a piece o' work. Probably reported me, but I never got an answer about it. She used tae whack us with a fuckin' ruler. We'd sit outside her office, snickering, thinkin' it was hilarious, but inside, it was a different story. You'd hear the lads shoutin' and screaming, and when yer turn came, ye knew ye were in for it. She'd lay into ye with that ruler, nae mercy, whackin' ye till yer hands were red and sore. She was a nasty cow, all right. And worse, she'd feel ye up under the guise o' a medical examination. She'd run her hands over ye in ways that made yer skin crawl. We were just kids, terrified and confused, but there was nae one tae turn to, nae one who'd listen or believe us.

As I dug deeper into the past, these memories would surface, raw and painful. They made me even more determined to find the truth, to hold those bastards accountable. I couldnae just let it go. I needed tae make sense o' it all, for masel' and for the others who suffered.

The NHS and none o' the doctors have ever apologised. I want the truth about what happened, but they wouldnae answer me. They just keep brushin' me off, treatin' me like an annoyance. It's infuriating. I want to ken why the Council took on child beaters to run their children's homes. How could they let such bastards be in charge o' us vulnerable kids? It's a disgrace.

The truth has tae come out sooner or later. These bastards canae just walk around free, pretendin' they did nae do anythin' wrong. But there's nothin' I can do; the people who abused me are all dead now. They can rot in hell for all I care. It does nae brin' me peace, though. Knowin' they'll never face justice in this life, it haunts me. Their deaths feel like a get-out-of-jail-free card. They never had to answer for what they did, never had to look me in the eye and acknowledge the pain they caused. I need the truth to come out, not just for me, but for all the kids who suffered at their hands. We deserve that much. The scars they left on us, physical and emotional, run deep. The least they could do is acknowledge it, even if they're no longer here to face the consequences.

WILLIAM SCATTERTY

The guy who ran the home I was in beat the shit out o' me, and the bastard went on tae work for the council. I was bounced off so many fuckin' walls when he hit me, it was a wonder I didnae break every bone in ma body. One day, he gave me a backhander, and I bounced off one wall tae the next.

When I finally had enough, I went doon tae the council offices, ready tae tear them a new one. By the time I was done yankin' that council tae pieces, there were about sixty people standin' at reception, and nae a single one moved. I stood there, fuming, and shouted, "Ye take on child molesters and child fuckin' beaters in yer children's homes. Why? Ye tell me why!"

They just stood there, silent, not a word between them. "I'm one o' the poor bastards he beat up, and I want the truth," I roared. "I'm goin' to fuckin' haunt ye when I die. When I pop ma clogs, I'm goin' to come and haunt you, drag ye off into the fires o' hell and watch ye burn. You'll lay there for the rest o' yer days."

ON AND OFF THE RAILS

I held the manager up by the throat, pinned him against the wall. He sort o' slid down, gaspin' for breath, until he was unconscious on the floor. The whole time, the receptionist stood on her desk, watchin' the show. She said she never had such a crowd, and nae one o' them dared to move.

Ach, I enjoyed maself, I tell ya! It felt good tae finally stand up to the bastards, even if they still refuse tae give me the answers I deserve.

The police turned up, but by then I had finished my rant. The bobby looked at me and said, "He can charge ye for assault." I shrugged and replied, "Ah yeah, that's fine. Take me tae court, put the cuffs on me, mate, I'll come down, but I'll read the fuckin' statement."

He gave me a long look and asked, "Is yer name Scatterty?" I nodded and said, "Aye." He then asked, "Who took a two-page statement?" Then he added, "Are ye in the Historic Child Abuse case?"

"Aye," I said again.

The bobby sighed and said, "Why dinnae ye just go home?"

WILLIAM SCATTERTY

I said tae the police, "When I die, I'm goin' to haunt ye bastards. Ye wouldnae be able to put handcuffs on me or put me behind bars!" Ye cannae let people walk away from the things they've done. Why the hell should they walk free? How many kids' lives have they ruined? I only put up wi' it for two years, so they didnae ruin my entire life, but there are kids whose lives they did ruin. Those poor kids had to fight on their own. I had to stick up for maself and them. But aye, I did go home.

The polis told me never tae harass the social workers, or I'd end up in court. I just want the truth, simple as. The bobby said, "Just dinnae go near them; they'll do ye for harassment, and ye'll end up wi' a jail sentence." I said, "I dinnae give a shit. Do it now then, get on wi' it." The bobby said, "To be honest, I cannae blame ye. What ye put up wi', it's not fair."

I was still determined tae get answers, so I phoned them up and said, "I want tae see them," and two o' them actually came here, tae my flat. They sat opposite me, all nervous-like, shufflin'

ON AND OFF THE RAILS

their papers. I leaned forward and said, "I hope ye two can fly because I'm thirteen floors up, dinnae try me!" They went white as sheets and stammered, "It was nothin' tae do wi' us, it's private and confidential."

I tell people what I think o' them, and if they dinnae like it, they can fuck off. I dinnae have time for their lies and cover-ups. I leaned in even closer and said, "Ye think ye can just hide behind yer desks and yer laws? I'm nae interested in yer excuses. I just want the truth. Simple as."

They were sweatin' bullets, clearly out o' their depth. It was clear they'd never faced someone like me before. I wasnae goin' to back down, and they knew it. I continued, "I've got nae patience left. I've lived through hell, and I'll nae let ye or anyone else sweep it under the rug. So, ye better start talking, or I'll make sure everyone knows what kind o' bastards ye are."

The room was so quiet, ye could hear a pin drop. They had no answers for me, just more bureaucratic bullshit. I told them straight, "When I die, I am goin' to haunt you, ye bastards. They wouldnae be able to put handcuffs on me or put me behind bars!"

"Ye canae let people walk away from these things they've done," I said, glarin' at the two tremblin' social workers. "Why the hell should they walk free? How many kids' lives have they ruined?"

Even as I walked them to the door, I made sure they knew I wasnae done. "I'll keep comin' back, I'll keep asking, I'll keep pushing. Because ye cannae erase the past, and ye cannae silence the truth. Not while I'm still breathing."

The battle for answers continues. It's nae just about me; it's about all the kids who were wronged. I'll nae let them be forgotten. They'll be sorry they ever messed wi' me. The truth will come out, one way or another. And when it does, I'll be there, watchin' them burn.

All the people who abused me are deid now. The social work department has pit a ban on me, sayin' I'm nae to contact or harass them. The polis threatened to arrest me if I did, but I said, "I'll harass the bastards as much as I want, mate." I just

ON AND OFF THE RAILS

want the truth. If they wouldnae tell me, they can tell the judge. When I die, I'll haunt those bastards. They'll be sorry they ever heard o' me. I want people punished for what they did to me.

Naebody has ever apologised or acknowledged the suffering. They just want to sweep it under the rug, pretend it never happened. But I wouldnae let it go. I'll keep demandin' answers until my last breath. And when I'm gone, I'll haunt those bastards, make sure they never forget. Ye canae erase the past, and ye canae silence the truth.

It's nae just about me anymore. It's about all the kids who suffered, who were beaten and abused, and had their lives turned upside down. The ones who had nae voice, nae power. I was lucky enough to survive, to come out the other side, but many weren't. I think about them every day, and it fuels my need for justice.

The truth has a way o' comin' out, no matter how deep ye bury it. I ken they'll keep tryin' to shut me up, to make me go away. But I'm stubborn, always have been. I'll nae be silenced, nae be ignored. They can ban me, arrest me, do whatever they want, but I'll nae stop. I owe it to those kids, to maself, to keep fighting.

So, I'll keep pushing, keep asking, keep demanding. Because the truth matters. Justice matters. And I'll make damn sure that those who wronged us will never be able to rest easy. Not in life, and not in death.

LESSONS AND REFLECTIONS

As I move intae the twilight o' ma life, I've come back tae Huntly, back tae ma roots. It feels right tae be here, where it all began. There's a sense o' peace in returnin' tae the familiar, the places and faces that shaped ma early years. Despite all the pain and the struggles, there's somethin' comfortin' about bein' back in the heart o' Aberdeenshire.

I've spent the last few years tryin' tae find a sense o' closure, tae make peace wi' ma past. It's nae been easy, but I've come tae realise that dwellin' on the hurt can only take ye so far. Now, I'm focused on livin' out ma final days wi' as much contentment as I can muster. I still have ma fight,

ON AND OFF THE RAILS

but it's tempered wi' a deeper understandin' o' life's fragility.

Ma niece Fiona, she's ma next o' kin. Her and her son are the only family I've got left. It's a strange feelin', havin' more family in the crematorium and the cemetery than walkin' about. We had a big family once, but now it's just me left on ma side. Fiona is Anne's girl, and she's been a pillar o' support, always lookin' out for me.

I'm still the same, though, I dinnae change. Somebody comes tae ma door, I say, "What the hell do ye want?" I've had a local councillor against the wall and ma neighbours came out and they said, "Has he upset ye, Bill?" and I said, "Well, slightly." They said, "I think ye better let him go, Bill, he's turnin' blue." "Oh, so he is." I let him go and he kinda slid down the wall. Nobody comes tae ma door. I mean, Jehovah's Witnesses, and I've spoken tae them. I said, "Do ye talk tae ghosts?" and they said, "No, we don't." I said, "Well, ye're talkin' tae me. Ye threw ma mum out because she gave me a blood transfusion," so I started windin' them up, sayin' I'm a ghost.

Despite everything, I've always been straightforward wi' people, never puttin' on airs or changin' how I speak. I cannae stand dishonesty. If someone bothers me, I let them know. That's probably why so few people come around anymore. I dinnae sugarcoat things. Life's too short for that kind o' nonsense.

Fiona is the only one who has time for me now. She visits when she can, always bringin' her son along. We sit and reminisce about the old days in Huntly, talkin' about how things have changed. I tell her stories about the family, the ones who are nae longer wi' us, tryin' tae keep their memories alive. It's a bit o' comfort, knowin' someone still remembers them.

I think about the old days often, back when the family was whole and we all lived close by. Huntly was a place where everyone knew everyone, and families stuck together. Now, it feels like those days are gone, and it's just me left tae remember them.

ON AND OFF THE RAILS

I suppose that's why I went back, tae be where ma roots are, even if most o' ma family are six feet under.

I wash some things in the world were back tae the fifties, sixties, and seventies because that's when everybody was together. There were nae problems; everybody mucked in. There were nae people standin' on the side lookin' in. All the kids played together. Ye get nothin' like that now. I live across the road from a housin' estate. I see kids goin' tae school, comin' home, and that's it. Ye only see them outside at weekends. Back in ma day, we were out from dawn till dusk, playin' games, gettin' into scrapes, and just livin' life. There was a sense o' freedom we had that kids today dinnae seem tae enjoy.

I wasnae affected by the child abuse in school; I didnae even know it was abuse. Back then, ye took yer licks and got on wi' it. We didnae think tae complain. Today, there's more awareness, and that's a good thing, but it also means that some o' the resilience we had tae build is lost. Kids are wrapped up in cotton wool now. They dinnae get tae experience the world in the same raw, unfiltered way we did.

Back then, the world moved at a different pace. People took the time tae talk tae one another, tae share stories, tae help oot. If someone in the village needed a hand, ye gave it without a second thought. Today, it feels like everyone is rushin', heads down, glued tae their screens. They've lost touch wi' the simple joys o' life. Ye'd be hard-pressed tae find a kid who knows the thrill o' buildin' a go-kart oot o' scrap wood or the satisfaction o' climbin' a tree and seein' the world from a different angle.

I've learned a lot from ma life, more than any school could teach. It's not been an easy path, but I've walked it the best I could. The world has changed so much from when I was a lad. Back then, there was a sense o' community, a sense o' lookin' oot for one another. Nowadays, it feels like everyone is oot for themselves.

ON AND OFF THE RAILS

Back in the day, we knew our neighbours. We didnae just live next tae them; we shared our lives wi' them. Ye could borrow a cup o' sugar or get help fixin' a broken fence. Now, people hardly know the names o' the folks livin' next door. It's all become so impersonal.

There's a lot tae be said for the simplicity o' the past. No constant bombardment o' information, no incessant noise from mobile phones and social media. Ye dealt wi' people face tae face, and that built stronger, more meaningful relationships. Kids today have all the gadgets, but they're missin' oot on real experiences. They dinnae know the joy o' gettin' their hands dirty in a garden or the thrill o' explorin' the woods wi' their mates.

In many ways, the challenges we faced back then made us tougher, more resilient. We didnae have the luxury o' givin' up when things got hard. We had tae push through, find solutions, and make do wi' what we had. That's a lesson that seems tae be lost on many today. There's a tendency tae expect everythin' tae be easy, tae be handed tae ye. But life doesnae work that way, and the sooner ye learn that, the better off ye'll be.

I've seen a lot in ma years, and I've learned that while times change, some things remain constant. The value o' hard work, the importance o' family, and the need for community. These are the things that truly matter, and they're what I hold onto as I look back on ma life and think about the future.

I mean, I'm still here. I go tae the hospital often enough. They call me "Wonder Boy" when I walk intae the hospital. I say, "Why do ye call me Wonder Boy?" They say, "Well, we wonder why ye're still fuckin' here!" I've had five heart attacks and four angina attacks. They say, "Ye should be fuckin' dead and up there." I say, "Ye dinnae want me up there; ma mother's up there, and she doesnae want me up there upsettin' the apple cart. That's why I'm down here in punishment." Doctors always say tae me, "Why are ye still here? Ye should be dead, gone. Nobody lives that long wi' five heart attacks, nobody!" I say, "Well, I am. I'm still fuckin' here!" He says, "Every time I examine ye, yer heart gets

ON AND OFF THE RAILS

stronger, but the rest o' yer body has given up." I say, "Well, there ye go then." I'm on five tablets a day: blood thinners, heart tablets, cholesterol pills, and another tablet tae keep ma heart monitored. They keep me goin'. Ye rattle me, I'm like an old tin can.

And so, as I face the days ahead, I do so wi' a sense o' gratitude for the life I've lived and the lessons I've learned. Huntly is where I'll spend ma final days, surrounded by the echoes o' the past and the hope for a future where the values I hold dear can find a place once more. I'll keep tellin' ma story, keep fightin' for justice, and keep livin' wi' the strength and resilience that has carried me this far. For in the end, it's the memories, the stories, and the connections that truly matter, and those are the things I'll carry wi' me, always.

I often reflect on ma journey, the highs and the lows. I think about ma wife, Angie, and ma son, Adam. They were ma world, and losin' them was the hardest thing I've ever faced. There's not a day that goes by that I dinnae think about them.

186

WILLIAM SCATTERTY

Sometimes, I feel them close by, and that brings me a bit o' comfort. Their presence in ma thoughts is a connection tae a time when life was filled wi' love and purpose.

Despite all the hardships, I've had good times too. I remember the camaraderie on the rails, the laughter, the friendships. Those are the memories I hold dear. I've been outspoken all ma life, never one tae mince ma words. It's probably rubbed some people the wrong way, but I dinnae care. I've always told it like it is, and I wouldnaechange that for anything.

I've also learned that it's important tae fight for the truth. I've spent years seekin' answers about what happened tae me and so many others. It's not been easy, and it's brought me into conflict wi' a lot o' people. But I'll keep pushin', keep demandin' answers. Because the truth needs tae be known. People today might think they're progressive, but they dinnae realise the importance o' facin' the past head-on and makin' sure the same mistakes arenae repeated. Ma two mates, Peter and John, are both

ON AND OFF THE RAILS

dead and gone now. I'm the only one left who can tell the story.

I dinnae know how much time I have left, but I intend tae use it well. I'll keep fightin' for justice, keep tellin' ma story, and keep livin' as best I can. Life has thrown a lot at me, but I'm still standin'. And as long as I'm here, I'll keep pushin' forward, one day at a time. The past has shaped me, and while the world around me has changed, the lessons o' those earlier days remain clear. Stick together, fight for what's right, and never lose sight o' who ye are.

There's nae doubt in ma mind that the world I grew up in was a better place. Aye, it had its share o' hardships, but there was a sense o' community back then, a bond among people that's sorely missin' today. We looked out for each other, helped one another in times o' need. The simple joys o' life were cherished, and there was a purity tae the way we lived.

Back in those days, a man's word was his bond. Ye could leave yer door unlocked and nae worry about anything. Neighbours were like extended family, always ready wi' a cup o' tea and a listenin' ear. It's a world I miss dearly, and I cannae help but wash that today's generation could experience that same sense o' camaraderie and trust.

In Huntly, I find traces o' that old world. The streets and fields remind me o' the boy I once was, runnin' wild and free, wi' a heart full o' dreams. It's a different place now, but the essence is still there if ye ken where tae look. It's in the smiles o' the old folks who remember the same days I do, in the laughter o' the bairns playin' in the park, in the quiet moments o' reflection by the river.

So, as I spend ma days wanderin' these familiar paths, I hold onto the belief that despite everything, I've lived a life worth livin'. The darkness I've faced has only made me appreciate the light all the more. And while I cannae change the past, I can choose tae find peace in the present, tae embrace the time I have left wi' a sense o' belonging.

Huntly will be where I make ma last stand, a place o' memories and reflections, a place where I

ON AND OFF THE RAILS

can finally lay down ma burdens and find some measure o' tranquillity. And as I look back on it all, I hold onto the hope that someday, the world might find its way back tae those simpler, kinder days.

Nephew Malcolm and his wife

My sister Anne and her husband John (with grandson Ryan)

Ryan, and his dad and mum. Ian and Fiona

Printed in Great Britain
by Amazon